Our Generation

"An observation of how the conflict between logic and emotion has shaped our world"

Aaron J Gough

Contents

Introduction

Chapter One – An Observation

Chapter Two – Defining Emotion

Chapter Three – Defining Logic

Chapter Four – The Internal War

Chapter Five – Mindfulness

Chapter Six – Social Media

Chapter Seven – Mental Health

Chapter Eight – God and Religion

Chapter Nine – The Natural World, And Us

Chapter Ten – A Future Perspective

Chapter Eleven - Love

Introduction

Everyone has a story. You will seldom find freethinkers in a world of limbic servants, like sheep carrying a message from one to the other, unable to think for themselves. Empaths drown in the monotonous sorrows of the spoiled. The ability of perspective lost in the winds of the indulgent, replaced by fruit from the poisonous tree.

No one is hated more that he who speaks the truth, so he remained silent, becoming the observer of the world around him, a lonely world through these eyes. Forever seeking satori.

Mother Nature gifted us with a sensory system to interpret and absorb the world around us. To feel its beauty and to realise what we are part of. There is a calming sense of wellbeing in the true realisation that we are part of this natural world that so many are seemingly ignorant to.

How do we interpret the world around us? Is it as simple as observing the things we see, matching an emotion to it and then moving on to the next scenario? Or, do we take the time to feel, to be truly present and really feel? To take a breath and observe our surroundings and interpret the beauty many seldom see.

Imagine walking up the street and without the distraction of thought. You are able to view and interpret your surroundings, uninterrupted and completely absorbing the world around you, the sunlight beaming off the edges of the leaves, the melody of the wind and the sound of your own heart. That singular energy source that science has shown us is omnipresent, a delicate beauty.

To be truly present in every moment is to attain a level of consciousness that disregards feeble thought. A challenge. Your reality neither speeds up nor slows down, it just is. The mind enters a realm of simultaneous adornment. Things appear to you in a frozen state of beauty that demands appreciation.

You are awake and aware of everything. Your current state of mind is a direct result of your ability to interpret your external reality. Your external reality is a projection of what your mind allows it to be and this in turn dictates your emotional state. Monotony is that of the unseeing.

This book is full of questions, theory and perspective. I wrote it neither to preach nor to tell people what to think, but to indulge in the act of thinking itself. Most of us in the modern day tend to follow, disabling our ability to be free thinkers.

Look around; we have a society of copycats and followers. Seldom do we come across a true original in a world of "sheeple". Such comfort in the realm of social acceptance, or is the fear of being you without the need of social approval too grand of an endeavor?

Not everyone has to see the world through your eyes. An issue that we have in society is that a lot of this generation believes that the world should adopt their personal principles and opinions to which in effect is dictatorship.

History reveals the human animal has in most cases been a follower. So is this behaviour relative? Or is it something that has led us astray? With the amplifying rise of social media, which is a shit-show of vanity and comparison, and a perfect combination for the onset of a multitude of anxiety-laden minds, we can observe extreme examples of innate behaviours that can help us on our quest to understand ourselves.

I wrote this book to highlight certain behaviours in society and it will inevitably cause debate, which is to be expected, as we are but an over-opinionated generation of idealists that contradict one another on a daily basis, whilst the clock ominously ticks on.

In truth, this book is full of what goes on inside of my own mind, my observations of society and the world around me and what is ultimately important to me, to which writing it down is a release.

By nature I am an observer and a ferociously deep-thinker. Pondering ego versus character, consciousness versus time and reality versus ideals.

My brain tends to pick up many details to which others miss. I am skeptical about the actions of others when I identify that those actions were projected based on emotional impulse rather than logic, especially when these actions have a decisive effect on our world.

I will be presenting my current views on a variety of subjects that will certainly get the backs up of those that have an emotional attachment to a specific topic. My advice to these people is to allow your mind to detach (partially) from emotion, and read these words with an open, non-biased mind. Become a blank canvas and allow the path of logic to be free from the obstruction of blind, impulsive emotion.

I do not know you, and you do not know me. I am not insulting you and this book should not be taken personally. I am addressing world subjects that we as a collective species should all be free to discuss. Nothing learned came from a lack of questions. The elephant in the room to which many are reluctant to address, will be addressed in great detail within these pages.

When critically discussing logic and emotion, it allows for a range of behavioural correlations to be observed and scrutinized from history, the modern day and the respective future. Patterns of human behaviour will be analysed.

The very act of critical and skeptical thinking, allows us to find truths that many will disregard and reject, regardless of how overwhelming the evidence is.
These folk are emotionally led and common behavioural traits will be both expected and exposed, usually in the form of a loud, rejecting outburst to which logic remains vacant.

Through out your day-to-day life you are faced with a multitude of social situations to which the reasons behind people's actions may seem odd and sometimes unexplainable. Sometimes the same can be said for our own behaviour. How hard it is to self-reflect and to be critical of our self when our dark ego is at the reins.

Impulsiveness, desire, greed and jealousy tend to be the drivers for such unexplainable and radical projections.

In an age where knowledge is freely accessible and in abundance like never before, we can propel ourselves in to becoming the very best version of ourselves. Find your flow state and liberate yourself. Nothing is unattainable and everything is within reach.

Empower yourself and never base your failures on the successes of others. I dream of a world where it is not rare to look in to the eyes of another and to see that they too are awake, present and aware of the world around them, where the difference between logic and emotion is understood.

They all glow with the colour grey, blank faces and vacant minded. A vibrant glow seldom seen, though hope is maintained. So many, disconnected from their greatest gifts. Would you rather be involuntarily aware of everything going on around you in detail, or live in the peaceful bubble of ignorance?

The latter, being the status quo. Compassion, the maintenance job for the freethinker. Humour being the only respite from all of the doors endlessly opening and closing, revealing all of the details of life.

So, I smile. Surfing the wave of distraction to escape the woes of deep thought, brought on by an involuntary interpretation of the external world, an endless rollercoaster of deciphering emotion for the reluctant Empath.

I await the sensory renaissance. The irony of never being alone, in such a lonely world. But for now, let us not appear crazy.

Where all humans are in touch with their gifted senses and can freely absorb their environment. Is this the vision of a dreamer? Long live the freethinkers. Although I may leap from example to example, everything that I write, orbits around the same point and subject matter, being human psychology, social philosophy and the human condition.

I have done my best to tie them together from a psychological standpoint. Apologies in advance for my candour and please, brace yourselves…

Chapter One

An Observation

We're fucked… For all of the beauty and carnage that we create I feel that humanity has become an enigma; this predominantly being due to humanity being prosperous yet unwise, beautiful yet at the same time ugly and ambitious although myopic in regard to its own longevity. How evident this is based on our endless yearning for more.

The planet we belong to was once an intense ball of flames, it was uninhabitable and hell like. Or am I getting my past and current state of humanity mixed up?

Though we are a miracle, we must learn to appreciate that many species came before us, are with us and will be here after us. Our self-imposed divinity is that of the ignorant. We must appreciate the ecosystems that protect the organism to which we are a part of. We are a danger to ourselves in a time where the natural order of things has been challenged.

I realise that was a brutal and somewhat intense opening, but I feel speaking openly and being utterly frank is perhaps what our generation needs. My candour is based on the importance of the bigger picture, to which most of us could not give less of a shit about as the ability to think long term is somewhat of a challenge for the innately short term thinker.

Our society is obsessed with chasing pleasures and validation. True depth is sacrificed for the easily relatable shallows of life, a world where greed has led to ignorance and low hanging fruit is in abundance.

Trends disappear almost as fast as they arrive, they the product of greed, over-indulgence and flawed self-projection based on the hunger for attention rather than genuine cause. It is the human attitude, you see.

A mindset of self-entitlement has left us servants to our limbic masters. Because of this attitude, we now live in a world where people with good intentions, are mercilessly silenced by the ruling, squealing few.

Of course, ideals in life are subjective to an individual. Society is not a dystopia for everyone as the realities of life differ from person to person. In fact, life has never been so good for the masses. For a huge percentage of the world population, we have more than we will ever need and liberties that many are without.

How evident this is in the world of social media where all have a voice to be heard. Yet in the minds of the many that have so much, they will forever be coming up short in one way or another. Purpose and life meaning can be established through the oddest of avenues when one is without.

Why is the idea of true prosperity and equality snuffed at and boiled down to a stigma of utopianism and idealism? Why do we not try to achieve the unachievable?

I suppose that the definition of prosperity is misconstrued in the mind of the myopic. There are many deep issues in our world that are only now starting to be addressed.

I think mentally, an evolutionary shift is occurring in some people and the successive generations are waking up to the idea of a necessary change. We can learn so much about ourselves from history, that we can see a time lapse of change occurring before our eyes. Views are changing and the balance of all things is sporadic.

We are all different and it is in those differences that we must appreciate each other. Our differences offer up new perspectives and open doors of understanding. The fact that we are all different is the one thing that we have in common.

Humanity has never been richer, healthier and more prosperous but yet we are still hungry for more. It is within this default-mindset that we can all learn to apply some changes that will pull us away from the toxic abyss of modern day hyper-convenience.

We as humans make choices every day and whether those decisions are based on logic or emotion will dictate the narrative in which you exist. Of course, life is supposed to be enjoyed and life is full of pleasures.

The issue is that we as humans tend to over indulge with everything that we do and the luxuries of life have drowned us in choices; those choices have led us to become weak, both emotionally and physically.
Of course, human variation dictates that we do not all operate in the same way. Indeed we are of the animal kingdom, but we are a sentient and often a rational animal.

In most cases, although opposing variables are evident, we have left behind the extreme examples of a Hobbesian state of nature. Though the internal selfish trait will forever exist, it is not our core trait as humans are adaptable and our nurture dictates our nature.

In these times of crisis we are effectively brought back a few decades in regard to the amount of time we have and in the energy we expend. We are seeing cases of a modern generation developing anxieties and depression through boredom. Highlighting the spoils of the modern day.

Boredom is the root of all creativity, it is said. I believe it is at the root of all chaos too.

In being confined to ones home during lockdown and becoming a victim to your own mind, drowning in time, who are you when the mind becomes still? How content are you without the conveniences of life? Did you feel that emotional impulse when imagining this? Like an impulsive, rejecting emotional reaction, a defense mechanism.

Time being the only true commodity that we have, it forcefully reveals a dire lack of meaning within the mind of those without. Without meaning our minds spiral in to chaos. To have meaning truly is everything. Finding and nurturing your meaning should be the pursuit of life.

When a deep sense of meaning or purpose is not realised in life, the void is filled with indulgencies. These indulgencies are short-term thrills that will need replenishing. Indulgence progression translates in to the term "Gateway".

Over exposure leads to discontentment and we become a hamster on a wheel chasing the never-ending pleasures of life only to feel empty regardless.

These are troubled waters to navigate yourself out of, although not impossible. Peeling back the layers of what you think summarises who you are as an individual can lead to some interesting revelations. This shit takes time and patience. The reasons why most are on the wheel their whole lives will become evident on this endeavour. A form of Darwinism one could argue.

I am going to highlight a few issues that stand out to me and they all revolve around freedom of preference.

Culture wars turn nation against nation and people against people. This is a distraction tactic used many times over throughout history. United we stand, divided we fall.

Ask yourself this, how many countries have you been to where the local people have been nothing but polite and welcoming to you? Finding common ground, humour and appreciation for each others culture is what usually occurs in my experience. We are all just people, living our lives and trying to survive.

It takes the implementation of suggestive thought to corrupt the mind of the average person. Control their emotions and you will control the person. Fear, religion and national identity are used as tools of manipulation. Why is the idea of peace but a dream? "Ubuntu" as it were.

Society certainly is vibrant with ideas at the moment. I notice some of these ideas turn in to movements to which I feel unsurprised by, due to the historical references of human behaviour that we have for comparison.
Hitler usually comes to mind when I hear the rants of these modern day hypocritical cults. Freedom is preached but freedom is not respected.

Even freedom itself has been expressed in such extreme forms that we are all forced to alter our preferences on such personal things, or face the harsh penalties of societies ridicule for not agreeing or for even being critical of an individual's choice.

I believe in freedom of choice for a person to do or be what ever they so choose. What I don't agree with is the hypocrisy to where my own freedom of opinion is either evoked or challenged.
I know that I was being vague, but that is because in truth, I don't care about what other people choose to do with themselves, I respect their right of choice. The fact

that I don't agree is neither here nor there, but remains my right to be so.

In some cases of freedom of expression, I struggle to remain impartial because I am forced to accept something about someone that they could not accept about themselves in the first place. Moving on...

Human beings have consumed meat and used animal products for survival since the very beginning. If we did not, we would not be here today. It is that simple. Anyone who tries to say otherwise is obviously leading with conjecture, an agenda based on the need to be part of something regardless of it's cause, or just an attention seeking, self-righteous fool.

If you choose to not be a consumer of animal products, I am cool with that as it is your choice to which you are entitled too. However, if you ever find yourself challenging the freedom of others to consume animal products, as is in their nature to do so, I would advise you check yourself before you are seen as a dictator, like Hitler.

I remember seeing a protest outside of a steakhouse in the UK. This particular steakhouse was owned and run privately by a man with a small family. This was his only source of income.
Due to the protest his business took a huge loss and in turn his family would have felt the strain. Now, this protest was happening mid-week and in the daytime. My instant thought was, do these people have jobs? Or do they spend their time hounding those who contribute to society in order to make themselves feel validated?

The psychology here is very interesting. They have a right to protest granted, but where is their moral compass? They feel animals are our friends and that they should not be consumed. That is fine with me, however I feel stopping a man from providing for his family outweighs the latter.

I suppose a lot of peoples actions are down to finding meaning in something, this being the most innate human chain of thought and pursuit.

The issue is that this pursuit often has detrimental effects to others that are ignorantly disregarded by the individual. I admire anyone that actively believes that they are trying to make the world a better place, but I question their wisdom in some cases.

In truth, there is no fairness in nature and life will never match the ideals of everyone. So trying to go against the grain to press your personal ideals on the rest of society will only cause conflict, thus creating a larger problem than what existed to begin with.

My advice would be to lead by example and live your ideals.
Those that feel inspiration by your example can make a choice to freely make their own changes too, based on the narrative you exhibit. By doing this you will also feel internal peace as you are only doing what you feel right.

Again, there will never be a time when we all agree on everything. Expressing your opinions in a logical way and without an emotional undertone will likely de-escalate the growth of a greater problem. We want to avoid opening Pandora's box.

Socrates said, *"I am the wisest man alive, for I know one thing, and that is that I know nothing"*. There is a huge lesson to be learned here and that is that we as a society must retain that, although we have our individual ideals, forcing these beliefs on the masses will only cause conflict.

This can be observed in many different regions of the world. We cannot be ignorant to this and allow ourselves to succumb to a belief that one way is the right and only way. What works for one person, may not work for another.

Finding meaning in forcing your beliefs on society is ignorant and narrow-minded. As humans we learn by example, so set examples rather than dictating them. Your ideals should not make others feel downtrodden.

Early on in this book I mentioned my belief that I feel a strong contender for the meaning of life, is to help others.
I believe that this is one of those things that play both in to logic and emotion. We all need help sometimes and nothing feels more rewarding than helping one another.

In all walks of life, but especially in this post Covid-19 world, hard times are going to be an issue for the masses. Redundancies and break-ups seem to be at the forefront of most people's problems. As the governments of the world scramble to salvage their economies, though people will inevitably suffer, we are the adaptable and based on our individual abilities to do so, will be evident in the outcome of our survival and resilience.

Sometimes, life doesn't go as planned and often our initial, default response is to shut down and become stagnant. But what does this achieve? We have to endeavor to create pathways of progression. By nature when things do not go our way we can become very emotional about it. This can cloud logic and in doing so, limit our abilities to keep moving forward and think of our options.

History is not short of hard times and history is also not short of showing us the resilience of the people. Even when all hope seems lost, there will always be path to take and foundations to rebuild on. In this instance we must take our time to think, think again and think even more so. How can you adapt as an individual? What else can you put your hand to? What do people need that you can provide? Even temporarily reducing rates for trade is better than remaining stagnant.

It is the act of perseverance that will carve out your route of progression and rebuilding your life, as you knew it.

You are a human and by that nature you are adaptable and have the ability to learn and turn your troubles in to your salvation. You must try to think local, identify the box in which you need to think outside of and in doing so, learn how to survive within the circumstances that life has bestowed upon you.

Children go to school in order to learn the fundamentals of life, as we know them, in order to survive and be able to understand the skills necessary to get through life. Perhaps a leaf can be taken from this as we all go through the hard times ahead.

The name of the game is survival. Putting your biases' aside and understanding that this is the time where all that matters is being able to provide for yourself and your loved ones is the main goal, perhaps some self-education wouldn't be to big of an ask. In doing so, it will speak volumes and you can stand with pride in knowing that you are doing all you can to find solutions to your problems.

The grind is always worth it and nothing worth having ever come to anyone without it. The grind makes you appreciate what you have so much more. You will never be worthless or helpless if you can accept this.

What is life without the little things? Living in the fast lane, unable to freely absorb the stunning world around you. That void in the mind that is present in all of us, often filled with alcohol, drugs or television, could rather be filled with the beauty that is life.

The industrial revolution took off with such speed that we are now in an age where we neglect the world around us with such stunning ignorance that I ponder the idea of how many people will one day sit on their death beds wondering where their time went.

History shows us how man has always gone with what is most profitable and with what brings him more things. In doing so, we have missed out on some true magic. Nature provided all yet we went with a different option that made us lose sight of a better way.

Over populated prisons and anarchy on the streets are all issues of lack of investment in the people. We have created an emotionally unstable and an emotionally led society. In some parts of the world where there is dire lack of opportunity and a huge reality of separatism, people have nothing to do.

They live in ghettos and often find themselves doing things that aren't good. Becoming shrouded in negative energy due to depression and a lack of worth based on having no meaning in life. In many countries they turn to drugs for relief and for synthetic happiness.

It suspends their reality. This creates a demand for drugs to which some see as an opportunity to earn money. This creates a vicious, negative and dangerous cycle, as the drug dealers will do all that they can to protect their income. Often resulting in murder and other crime. You see how the problem grows?

If governments were to create opportunity, ones that create income for their people, this problem could be avoided. When highlighted in this manner, it is understandable as to why people do what they do. Byproducts of all of the above create social tensions that can evoke tribal like behaviour, leading to gangs and more violence. The whole process creates natural enemies amongst people.

Division allows for people to be controlled. Getting to the route cause of the problem is plain to see and easy in theory. However in practice this is not the case. Government funds that should be going to the welfare of their people do not seem to find the way there.

I accept that the world will never be an ideal place, but we can at least endeavor to try and make it so.
With every thought and observation that I have, I always face confliction within my own mind.

When mentally dividing world problems between logic and emotion, it is difficult to find peace of mind. While writing this book, I have sat at many tables and drank coffee in many different places, from Dubai to London,

Cape Town South Africa, Copenhagen and Lisbon. Observing people from all walks of life.

I also remember writing about when visiting foreign countries, of how welcoming and kind the local people are. So far, this has certainly been the case. Rather than coffee, I find myself drinking Rooibos tea and gifted a smile by a passer by or two.

Culturally diverse and a delicate place, although I feel safe, it is not hard to sense that this place is a tinderbox to which the slightest spark could trigger off some extreme occurrences.

Staring out of a window, past a red and white lighthouse, I can see Robben Island, which was where the late Nelson Mandela was imprisoned.

I cannot help but think about the mindset of this man and appreciate his visions for the future. This was a man that had all of his rights taken away from him, a man that had to endure a lack of physical freedom but yet found his mental freedom.

Subsiding his emotions, or maybe embracing his emotions and being able to think freely and productively whilst incarcerated is a testament to what this book is about. That is, being a mindful and intended separation between logic and emotion for the greater good. He understood that, for the country he loved to progress, he must unite the people.

Black, white and mixed raced people, had to be united for the greater good. This was a huge endeavour and one that was not fully achievable as can be felt around town today. Sadly, the logic of Nelson Mandela was not enough to conquer the emotions of the masses. Corrupted and ignored by those that succeeded him, the divisions in society are still very much visible.

The eyes speak in South Africa and there is a seedy undertone when walking the streets. Opportunity is scarce and poverty is rife. Emotion is high and tensions are visible as the wounds of the past are still very much open. Every day, I see a homeless man by a bus stop.

He paces endlessly up and down, looking at the ground. His hand holding his chin as he paces, I wonder what he thinks about. He does this for hours at the same spot every day. He checks the same two bins every few minutes. He has routine and he has built habits.
I wonder if his predicament is that of his own doing or that of his government failing to create opportunity for its people.

I wonder if this man is able to turn his life around or if it is too late. I am not naive however I do ponder the idea of how someone in this situation could turn it around. I think of the action needed to turn this place in to a utopia.

I went to a comedy show whilst in Cape Town, and I picked up on a point a local comedian said. He said that the only thing that unites South Africans is sport.

Sport triggers of a huge emotional reaction, it triggers off excitement, unity and a sense of belonging. Therefore emotion is what both unites and divides people in this instance. When the sporting event is over, times return to those of old and the wounds of the past are felt again.

I had a conversation with a local person here recently, this man happened to be mixed race. His view was that even when presented with opportunity, those less fortunate squander it. A shortsighted agenda is all that is known.

My response was that if a long term agenda was presented and understood, perhaps the opportunities presented to the less fortunate people of this society would be realised. Immediately he told me that their brains do not work this way and that it is almost like they are not evolved to this extent mentally.

This was hard for me to mentally digest however I did not want to dismiss his view. Perhaps some more subtle and respectful wording would have been better but who am I to say that. I have not lived in this country and my understanding is that of an outsider.

Of course, this did trigger off a pattern of deep thought and reflection on the conversation I just had. For me, the various colours that humanity comes in, is beautiful. It should not divide us. Disliking someone for the colour of his or her skin is pig headed.

Are the white people in England different to the white people in America? Most would argue yes. When put to me that the black people in South Africa are different to the black people in England, it initially made me feel very uncomfortable. Growing up in a very diverse part of the world, colour was not an issue where I grew up.

So an immediate conflict occurred in my mind as I struggled to understand the opinion of this individual. Of the cuff it does sound like a racist comment, and the immediate emotional response contradicts the point. I took some time to think about it.

I came to the conclusion that in South Africa, for the most part, black people are the majority who live in squalled conditions, they are the ones who tend to initiate conflict, but what this does not do is make it okay to judge all black people as though they are no good. This would be racist and small-minded.

Different regions yield different troublemakers and the colour of their skin is just based on region, it is simply relative. Venezuela yield an abundance of troublemakers that are of local and Latino origin, my own country has troublemakers of all backgrounds. So in this sense, I do understand that regionally, the black people here are different to the black people found elsewhere.

It is a difficult subject to navigate. The fact that these people are black should be neither here nor there. Unfortunately however, it is the case in this part of the world. A sad truth that easily is subject to debate, though having seen and experienced this first hand as someone who is not racist and of a very open mind, it is difficult for me to form a counter argument when something is so apparent.

Of course we can look at the reasons at to why the situation is the way it is here, but we find ourselves oscillating around something in which we see around the world time and time again. Social divisions implemented by those in power to allow for ease of control amongst its people. Attacking the emotional mindset of different sects of people to play them against each other is something so prominent in this world.

Nelson Mandela had a vision of a rainbow nation. He was detached from the material world and was gifted with eyes that were wide open. It is a sad truth that his vision was not enough to inspire his successors to change the world.

I find that in my own life experiences, greed is a very prominent thing and humans are always able to sugar coat their intentions when they are behaving this way.

Ultimately, it is the behaviour of all peoples as a collective that dictates the narrative. The colour of skin and behaviour that is projected is relative to where that person is from in the world. The behaviour itself is of no unique trait to any specific race or region as we see all behaviours in all regions of the world. Humans often pick out differences in each other for detriment.

Chapter Two

Defining Emotion

Although there is currently no scientific consensus on a definition for emotion, there have been many interpretations. We feel what emotion is, but do we understand it? Emotional trauma has the power to alter the life and outlook of an individual.

Many people do their very best to hide these damages, but over time they tend to come to the surface in one way or another. Some have been involved in no personal trauma themselves; though suffer from an amygdala hijack as though they were. I define this as phantom trauma. I will get more in to that later.

Decisions are made based on an individual's current state of mind at any given time. Their behaviour is governed by their simultaneous emotional state. A calm mind observes with ease, when a busy mind is blind.

Up until recently, I had an understanding of emotion with which I was satisfied. I believed, that all human beings had an emotional brain and a logical brain. To which with the application of self-discipline and practice, we could learn to understand and differentiate between.

We could learn when we are reacting to stimulus emotionally and try to utilise logic for a better outcome. This of course would be a maintenance job. Differentiating between logic and emotion allows for the exposure of much bullshit in life and allows us to give it the swerve. I have come to the conclusion that all humans have opposition within their minds.
Most are unaware of it.

In becoming aware of it, there are those that can become confused, angry and mentally unwell. Some prosper from the realisation and benefit from a vision due to newfound mental clarity.

We have the ability to feel two ways for one thing. We can feel one way emotionally and another way for it logically. Emotion usually dominates over logic and this is evident in today's world. The limbic system is the part of the brain responsible for emotional and behavioural response and we have become illogical slaves to it.

This opinion of mine was recently challenged, and rightly so. Based on there being no official agreement on the definition of emotion, why not accept a challenge that could further my own understanding?

The challenge came from someone whose name I will not expose out of respect. She is an academic and a psychological intellect. Though she suffers greatly from anxiety herself, I feel this drives her attainment for understanding of the human condition.

She put it to me, in a rather large number of words that logic itself is derived from emotion. That all humans react to all stimulus emotionally, that we process the emotion and then apply the logic required, as though we are solely an inlet and receptor of emotion, and secondly a logical thinker.

This made sense to me, however it felt incomplete. I was unsettled by this hypothesis. I knew there were many examples in history of circumstances that showed where emotional stimulus led to no rational form of logic. In fact I recalled situations I had been in personally where this was the case.

Having responded with this, she told me that it appears we have a different definition of logic. After spending some time together and observing the nuances of each other's personalities and having the opportunity to point out where my original point was evident in her own behaviour, we quickly came to realise something quite obvious. All humans are different.

By nature humans adapt to individual circumstances, be those circumstances positive or negative. Some humans are emotionally led, have deep emotional attachments to particular things and the path of logic is completely blocked. Any suggestion that contradicts their personal view is rejected, sometimes aggressively and irrationally.

Others, have the ability to decipher between logic and emotion, but will ignore the logic to bend the knee for emotion, which I would define as emotional servitude. This is usually based on traditions or paternal beliefs that have been passed down.

Some have the ability to think logically in most cases, regardless of external or internal stimulus. Emotion is seen as chaotic and unproductive. These people tend to be introverts, but not always.

Psychopaths have the ability to display emotion as though they are of a regular mental disposition, though they feel nothing other than curiosity and are the deepest of minds.

Human variation allows for no definitive order of working for the human mind, collectively.
There is however the common mind, to which we can use as a guide of general understanding.

Although I have stated that the variables are vast, I will be referring to the common mind throughout this book. Generally speaking, most human beings in the modern day tend to be highly emotionally reactive to the day-to-day social stimuli of life.

Emotion governs modernity. We are hardwired to do things in order to bring ourselves happiness.

Naturally, most of us trot around as emotional inlets to society and the world around us. Our expectations sit high and we are receptive and reactive to anything that falls short of them. When high expectations are not met, disappointment usually occurs.

This disappointment leads to unhappiness. In this perspective, your happiness is contradicted by your self-implemented expectations. Maintaining point zero expectation is unrealistic and delusional. As a human, such rigour is unattainable. Being mindful and being able to anticipate that in most cases your expectation will fall short will help in the long-term filtration of happiness.

Oxymoronically, never lose enthusiasm or optimism. The finity of life demands appreciation of every moment.

The issue is that short-term and long-term happiness is misunderstood and due to many modern day conveniences and expectations of life, we have lost our discipline to work hard and to be patient when seeking true fulfillment. In seeking happiness for the long-term, many find themselves slaves to the short-term.

Naturally, most of us trot around as emotional inlets to society and the world around us. In the relentless pursuit of happiness and fulfillment, society is obsessed with validation from others rather than becoming emotionally whole and stable internally.

The smog of faux-liberal society in the modern day clouds true logic. It is utterly and impulsively emotion based for self gain. The communication plane is blocked due to arguments for self-validation. Purpose and meaning is found in low hanging fruit.

Humans hunt for emotion, they seek it and they yearn for it. The same way a dog returns the ball back to you, expectantly looking at you to throw it again. Emotional ping pong if you will. Or "wif-waf" if your name is Boris Johnson. What happens when you stop throwing the ball?

Emotion, be it positive or negative should be viewed as a whole. When you react to something, positively or negatively, you are feeding it. By removing your emotion from a situation, you remove yourself completely.

You simply stop playing the game.

In times of heated emotion we can become lost in troubled waters. Blindly feeding the problem and succumbing to self-sabotage. Having invested so much of our self in to something, that the loss is felt as though part of our self has perished.

The emotions of humanity have become far more complex than those of our ancestors. Based on the conveniences of modernity, we have freed up much of our mental space from worry of not eating and where is safe to sleep at night, to that of social expectation. This comes with a plethora of frantic consequence.

Survival has become superficial.

Fear is implemented as a tool of control to which binds us to the status quo. We fight amongst each other blind-sided to what really matters. Homophobia, racism, religious wars and sexism all used to turn us on one another.
This plays in to the negative side of human emotion and clouds the path of logic. Are there answers as to why we always have to fight each other over such things or is it just relative?

Common folk argue endlessly with each other over things that will always exist and are the direct collective reaction to when the mighty and magical spotlight of the media highlight specific differences that are relative and beautiful in society. Portrayed in a manner that is suggestive, in order to create divisions. This causes civil unrest, in what would otherwise be a peaceful society.

Problems amongst society exist, they always have and they always will. When large volumes of people of different backgrounds and traditions live amongst each other, there will inevitably be conflict. Though we play in to this psychological trick, ego led and full of anger. Slight of hand at its finest.

The devils greatest trick was having you believe that he doesn't exist.

Our behaviour is to blame, our weak-minded, sheepish attitude to which leads us to impulsively rise to any provocation that pertains to us personally. We mindlessly react emotionally to subjective stimulus, rather than forming a personal opinion based on your own logic.

Professor Lisa Feldman Barrett is a Canadian Psychologist at Northeastern University. She is known for the theory of constructed emotion.

Her studies have brought her to the theory that your brain does not react to the world by only experience, but by predictions. She explains that emotions are guesses in relation to past experiences and that by cultivating your emotional intelligence you can become the architect of your experiences.

People always need something to latch on to and become expressive about. This is in our DNA and part of who we are. We are socially dependent creatures as evolution has shown us. When many feel alone they seek the company of others via any conduit available.

These vulnerable people are impressionable and will follow a crowd even if they do not fully understand the narrative. They are just happy to be part of something and to feel acceptance.

This has led to many issues in our world, where once an idea or concept has been implanted, the masses will latch on to it, creating divisions amongst the public sector. Like puppets being emotionally controlled, blind to the hand up their arse. Slight of hand at its finest.

The implementation of emotional based divisions in the public sector is no new trick and one that will never cease to prevail for the agenda of the elite.

Many have eyes but they do not see. This shortsightedness has led to outbreaks of civil unrest and is usually dominated by issues that we can all agree on are not acceptable but otherwise highlighted as a distraction to something else. As mentioned earlier in this book, once you control the emotions of an individual, you can control their actions.

Like a hamster on a wheel we go around and around to no end. The sheer abundance of human opinion creates a permanent variation of beliefs that will never align. This has to be accepted to some extent. Finding an external balance in society will never occur, as this contradicts the former.

Finding internal balance will be based on the acceptance that humanity will always differ in opinion and belief. To which only you can mentally come to the conclusion and accept that you can do nothing about it. You must create your own peace based on the understanding that some things are not within your control.

Control is what humans seek innately. A challenge to this need for control is followed in most cases by a projection of a default emotional reaction, thus creating chaos. The remedy to this is at the root of the problem. Learning to apply logic in the form of understanding our own limitations in any given situation is where we will discover our liberation.

Becoming mentally free is no small feet and the pursuit of the wise. Within all of our minds, we have all faced those cliché challenges of knowing that we have to do something progressive, but taking the easy route in letting the moment pass by means of procrastination.

A missed opportunity to cease control over ones own mind. A lack of self-discipline allows these moments to build up, in turn making you weaker and weaker. You become emotional and blame the world for not giving you the life that you want, the life you feel you deserve. You see others doing well and feel bitter, endlessly searching for excuses.

If you have it in you to self-reflect and observe your life choices without an emotional bias, taking self pity and relying on excuses as to why things haven't gone your way, you will be able to see that the situation you have found yourself in is entirely based on your own inaction.

What is pain? To me, pain is an immediate response to a given situation. Be it physical or emotional. In this instance, I would like to focus on the emotional.

Emotional pain comes from situations that are both within your control based on the decisions you have made leading up to a specific situation, and also situations that are completely out of your control like the death of a loved one. Emotional pain is difficult and can be extremely intense. Leading to outbursts of uncontrollable energy and feelings of desperation.

Pain in itself fades with time but in the given moment feels as though it will last forever. Pain is essential for growth. It is in essence, life experience to which can lay strong foundations of emotional resilience. Like a vaccination, over time you become stronger and immune to lesser bullshit.

However, there will inevitably be those times where life will dish some serious drama your way to which although you may be able to think calmly and logically in the unfortunate situation, you will be in constant battle with your emotions. This is what makes you human. Pain is shit.

The arrow of time is unstoppable and will forever move forward, times will change and new things will come in to your life that tend to make the past a little hazy and easier to manage. Therefor embracing the arrow of time is an important thing to remember when enduring the pains and the trials of human life.

Many humans attach a behavioural trait to themselves as though this is the sole way in which they think. "I am a realist!" comes to mind, however this is a mere trait of general human behaviour and when expressed in this manner, allows one to feel emotionally superior to some extent, or perhaps a simple way of processing something that would evoke unwanted but necessary emotions, they say this as though they are incapable of seeing things in the innate way nature has gifted them to see things.

All humans feel a grand spectrum of emotion, it is just that some humans are able to accept and be content with the fact. Pain, when unaccepted can lead to fear. Fear of pain can lead to anxiety, and anxiety is an issue that we see quite widely in the modern day.

Anxiety ridden people are left, right and center. There is even medication to mask it. The fact is that humans are supposed to both feel and embrace the full spectrum of the emotional gambit. We are supposed to learn and grow from our emotions.

In doing so, we become mentally strong and dare I say it, evolved. Now, masking this evolution will create a generation of people that are ill equipped and incompetent in dealing with issues that life will throw at them. The world will never be a safe place as a whole, and to the same extent that you will suffer if you cannot survive financially, if you cannot survive emotionally, the world will swallow you whole.

People will take advantage of you. The best medicine is preparation and this can only come via the conduit of good parenting and having teachers that are in touch with their "realist side".

In truth, we can only strive to create our own perfect "local" world. If this is done, then as a collective we could see some improvement in the global world. I truly believe that pain is essential for growth, to the same extent that failure is part of success.

The issue we face is that when people feel, but do not understand, it is almost impossible to enable them to understand.

You see, when someone is connected to something emotionally, they give it meaning and purpose. They enable an object or a thing to hold power and in doing so, it holds power over them. Objects that humans dumb-willingly use, and allow them to hold influence over their emotions.

Our emotions are untamed and forever impulsive, the wild stallion of the mind. They can be beautiful, painful and intense. Emotion is the strongest force within the human mind, yet so easily corrupted and influenced. Any form of emotional intelligence is to be applauded.

I am not trying to demonise emotion. I believe it is what emits human compassion and altruism. Emotion is responsible for a lot of good in the world and some of the strongest connections that defy logic.

Our emotions are of our default mindset, part of our survival and the very foundation of what makes us human. Without emotion, logic is chaos.

People always need something to latch on to and to become expressive about. This is in our DNA and part of who we are. We are socially dependent creatures as evolution has shown us. When many feel alone they seek the company of others via any conduit available.

These vulnerable people are impressionable and will follow a crowd even if they do not fully understand the narrative. They are happy to be part of something and to feel acceptance. This has led to many issues in our world, where once an idea or concept has been implanted, the masses will latch on to it, creating divisions amongst the public sector.

Like puppets being emotionally controlled, blind to the hand up their arse. Slight of hand at its finest. The implementation of emotional based divisions in the public sector is no new trick and one that will never cease to prevail for the agenda of the elite. Many have eyes but they do not see.

This shortsightedness has led to outbreaks of civil unrest and is usually dominated by issues that we can all agree on are not acceptable but otherwise highlighted as a distraction to something else. As mentioned earlier in this book, once you control the emotions of an individual, you can control their actions.

Like a hamster on a wheel we go around and around to no end. The sheer abundance of human opinion creates a permanent variation of beliefs that will never align. This has to be accepted to some extent. Finding an external balance in society will never occur, as this contradicts the former.

Finding internal balance will be based on the acceptance that humanity will always differ in opinion and belief. To which only you can mentally come to the conclusion and accept that you can do nothing about it. You must create your own peace based on the understanding that some things are not within your control.

Control is what humans seek innately. A challenge to this need for control is followed in most cases by a projection of a default emotional reaction, thus creating chaos. The remedy to this is at the root of the problem.

Learning to apply logic in the form of understanding our own limitations in any given situation is where we will discover our liberation. Becoming mentally free is no small feet and the pursuit of the wise. Within all of our minds, we have all faced those cliché challenges of knowing that we have to do something progressive, but taking the easy route in letting the moment pass by means of procrastination.

A missed opportunity to cease control over ones own mind. A lack of self-discipline allows these moments to build up, in turn making you weaker. You become emotional and blame the world for not giving you the life that you want, the life you feel you deserve. You see others doing well and feel bitter, endlessly searching for excuses.

If you have it in you to self-reflect and observe your life choices without an emotional bias, taking self pity and relying on excuses as to why things haven't gone your way, you will be able to see that the situation you have found yourself in is entirely based on your own inaction.

Chapter Three

Defining Logic

Logic is the silent voice of reason, the processor of our external world and circumstances. Logic is the internal negotiator of emotion, the charmer to the cobra. Logic can in most cases, be the order out of chaos. Looking back over millennia we have observed how freethinkers have used calculated logic to achieve their ideals. Throughout history we can observe the examples set when an individual was able to suspend emotional impulse and free the path of logic for an optimal outcome.

In most cases, logic is silent. When able to process a situation logically, ambient understanding occurs and the best course of action or inaction is taken. Logic is not to be confused with knowledge. Knowledge is the attainment of information. Logic is the ability to mentally process any given situation with clarity.

With logic comes a calm and sentient mind. The ability to view situations from multiple perspectives becomes easier as emotion is not blocking the path. When the mind is calm, we become an inlet for all of the beauty of the natural world. We simply feel, we simply be.

We progressively regress to a simpler way of thinking, unobstructed by the monotony of modernity. Shedding the cumbersome weight of social expectation and in turn growing from within. Logic is the gateway to consciousness, which holds the key to enlightenment.

Weeding is a maintenance job even in the most tended to of gardens. Maintaining complete logic is an impossible endeavour and no human is of such rigour. By nature we are flawed and only the perspective of the observer holds perfection. It is in the acceptance that our logic will often be obscured by emotion that we realise and become aware of the faults in our behaviour.

This suggests that logic is an ever-evolving concept and internally we are all, always learning from our experiences and mistakes.

Your outlook on any given situation is the product of your perception and ability to think long and short term. Poor judgment tends to be based on impulsive decisions where all logic is absent. It is not quite the same thing as normalcy bias, but yet still an example of a default and untrained mind. Decision-making is an art.

Taking the time to logically process a situation and to weigh up your options with a calm mind is only acquired through discipline and often exposure. This is all done by choice and is a conscious decision to decipher a problem with clarity. Ignoring all external distractions is a challenge, but you will see that others will realise your ability to think constructively when it is required.
Many are intimidated by this and in some instances, some will even try to hurry you along as they cannot contain their own emotions and be patient for your answer.

In this, you will subsequently learn how feeble the minds of some can be. It is not of your concern and it is not for you to justify or explain your methodology of thinking. All you can do is explain yourself in a manner that is understood. Calibrating your language for a specific individual enhances communication skills.

Disconnecting from a conventional default mindset is no small task and requires the attainment of patience. In suppressing impulsive emotional reactions for one that is logical, you will find yourself coming to many conclusions based on your newfound clarity of thought and comparative, perspective-based thinking. However, although you may come to conclusions on common issues, you will find that it falls on deaf ears in most cases when expressing an opinion.

This is where the normalcy bias is evident in society, as you will observe time and time again. You will view the world through new eyes and be astounded at how robot-like many people are. Almost like worker ants. This offers up a level of predictability in some cases and in turn gives you comprehension on some situations not being worth your emotional investment.

Where there are pros there are always cons. If logic is sworn by, and emotion is forcefully ignored and shelved, even when felt, perceived evil can occur. What is logical is not always what is correct.

This may sound contradicting but I feel it is a necessary perspective. For example; I am of the belief that by human perspective, there is no fairness in nature.

Is it fair that male pigeons in their droves will chase a female pigeon to mate with her whilst she is trying to get away? Is it fair that a male lion will kill cubs when taking over a new territory?
Although we may see the logic in the chaos of nature, we still feel uneasy about these things emotionally. We feel sadness. What is fair is relative.

Of course there are many examples in nature that do not sit well with human emotion. If there is no fairness in nature, is it right for humans to oppose nature?

Is there logic in this? Now, obviously as humans we have different social understandings to other species of animal. We have innate human virtue which prevents this kind of behaviour being socially accepted, and rightly so. Understanding behaviour is not condoning it.

If I asked two people to draw a picture of a cup that was in front of them, would I receive the same drawing from both people? Would either one of the drawings be wrong? Of course not, both drawings would be of the same thing, emitting the same message, but from different perspectives.

Now imagine the same scenario in a world of almost eight billion people and rather than drawing a cup, drawing on issues of humanity.

Now can you understand the importance of listening and paying attention to one another rather than arguing over whom is right?

The variation of perspective amongst the vast number of humans alive today, will ensure that life will never match the ideals of everyone and that perfection is but the personal perspective of an individual.
This crudely proves that humanity, will never find harmony with itself on a macro level.

However, if we can accept this, it will allow for a path of understanding, appreciation and additionally some would argue is more important, a path of learning from another perspective.

A prominent issue in society is that of the closed mind. The closed mind that is not ready to see or listen to the perspective of another. The level of difference it could make to the circumstances of an individual are huge, if this simple way of thinking was understood. Arguing over perspective is not constructive and often both perspectives are correct, but presented differently.

My point is to highlight the difference between logic and emotion. Logic will always be the voice of reason, the voice we should lean towards in troubled times. But without emotion, logic is chaos.

It has been the task of my life to learn how to harness a calm mind and to think before I allowed my emotions to project in to physical form. Although a maintenance job, the outcome is always better. You must do what is necessary but also do what is beneficial for you in the long term.

Endeavor to play the long game, not the short game. Be disciplined and train your mind to be a formidable tool for self-progression.

Having come from very little and going to five different high schools I struggled very much to realise my own mental capacity. I was riddled with emotion. I come from a small troublesome corner of South West London where gangs and knife crime were rife.

Times were extremely hard and leaving school at the start of a recession made things even harder. Feeling social pressures and broken home depression, life was one big anger fueled time bomb waiting to explode.

I felt so much pressure that I did some crazy shit just to get by. Life was tormenting. After a while I realised that someone always had it worse and that I needed to appreciate my problems. I began to observe the world around me, and my place within it. Watching the social behaviours of others whilst watching the vast colours of human emotion float around like an ambient rainbow, it was beautiful.

I learned to love people and how truly fragile we all are. I listened to people having conversations in other languages that I didn't understand at the time, but based on their body language I could grasp the tone of it.

I began to realise that the world is huge and far bigger than the one that I lived in mentally. I started to read non-fiction books, anything I could learn something from. I began learning Spanish, becoming obsessed with information about anything.

I was enjoying education for the first time in my life and I just couldn't get enough of it. Self-education is bliss and I disregard and try to correct anyone that says they cannot do something or achieve something.

It is a state of mind and the application of will power. Patience is the most difficult faculty to master. Plato said that all learning is remembering. The information is not what is difficult; it is the untrained faculty of remembering that needs to be established. In short, you must learn how to remember, to remember. Lost you?

It was this pursuit of self-discovery that enticed me to challenge myself and focus on harnessing a calm and observant mind, non-reactive to social torment and solely interested in listening rather than speaking. Allowing others to empty their emotional tanks so that the mind was open and easier to engage with. People can learn a lot from themselves when they pay attention. Self-reflection is key.

My mind became a sponge and no topic was uninteresting and no person was unworthy of my time. The world opened up to me. As the years progressed I became intrigued with events and issues that were going on in the world. I came to the conclusion that although the world is such a beautiful place, it does unfortunately have many issues, too many for one mind to comprehend without going completely insane.

Reiterating an earlier statement that patience itself is difficult to master, once we do the world around us glistens and opportunities of self-development become endlessly apparent. In this noisy world in which we live, surrounded by convenience, our prospects of self-development become limited. We are blinded by our vices. Drowning in a world of indulgence.

How many times have you heard someone say, "I could never learn a language" or something similar? Which is an immediate cancellation of any prospect to acquiring a new skill. We as humans are learning machines and history has shown us this. All that is necessary is the will itself to learn. Having the understanding that although laborious, the attainment of a new skill outweighs the graft required.

Once we master this, we realise that we can learn anything and that we can achieve anything.
By nature we make a lot excuses for ourselves, this is usually due to the cerebrum (the thinking brain), doing everything necessary to appease the limbic brain (your emotional brain). However, if we understand this we can then apply discipline. We can teach ourselves to operate differently and within a productive cognition that allows us to live a progressively better and more fulfilled life.

The potential we have once we obtain this will be true cerebral evolution. Patience and discipline will arm you with the focus and consistency required to achieve everything that you have ever wanted. Coupled with a healthy lifestyle you will glow.

Looking after your body is something you are completely responsible for. You cannot blame the government nor society for what you decide to put in to your body. Passing the blame is easy and that of a weak mind. Seizing responsibility and making the necessary changes within your diet is a good first step in to changing the usual processes of your brain.

Your body is constantly renewing itself, cells are renewing even as you are reading this. What you consume regularly will dictate how healthy your body will be in the future. It is not about starving yourself, but about setting a caloric limit and ensuring you are eating nutritionally dense foods, drinking plenty of water and getting good quality sleep. Watch your life improve…

It is very tiresome to see many people developing health conditions due to a lack of dietary education and/or discipline. Masking symptoms with medication, like using a pair of scissors to cut away weeds and not pulling them from the root. Hippocrates said "Let food be thy medicine and medicine be thy food". Truer words seldom spoken.

Every aspect of your life is completely within your control. Nature will provide all, and the modern day of technological advancement makes it more so easier. Develop your habits, develop your principles and evolve. Help as many people as you can, cheer strangers on and smile more, because the world can use some more good. In doing so, you will inevitably improve your quality of life and people will gravitate towards you.

Our reality is created in our minds. We can change our reality by changing our mind. Plato also said this and every time I read it my mind goes in to a deep wonder.

If by default, the idea that any form of self-discipline is a bad thing, rejected and seen as a threat by the limbic brain, then it is in this root of this understanding that we can apply soft, subtle changes that over time will improve life as a whole.

We come home and watch TV, We travel to work and put the radio on or our headphones in, we work in front of a computer screen, we become so drained from this meaningless cycle, that towards the weekend we go out to party and find ourselves at the bottom of a bottle and a bag to 'relax'.

Where is the time to look within? And process how we truly feel and to find our own meaning. It may sound like I am against the vices of life, which couldn't be further from the truth. I enjoy weekends out just as much as the next person, the difference is that I don't use going out as an escape. I am not blind to my own meaning. By nature we are social creatures, but if that obsession with a social lifestyle is built on weak foundations, we will see a mental collapse at some point.

Chapter Four

The Internal War

Logic and emotion have been at war in every human mind from the very beginning. Emotion is the relentless victor in most cases. Our emotions are the strongest force we are capable of projecting in to the world and they take many forms.

What Heidegger described as "ontic" is what means everything to the masses. They say that the wolf that wins is the wolf that you feed. Mentally, if we feed the wolf of worry, chaos will ensue. Emotional reactions get the better of those of logic in most cases, making you weak and allows for others to also feed your wolf.

The power of suggestion to the malleable mind allows emotion to block their logic and this is evident in society today. Order and structure are essential for the masses that know innately only disorder. This faux-dystopia is blind to the details of Occam's broom, and perhaps this is a good thing.

Once we apply logical thought, like a snake charmer we are able to tame our emotions. Being able to articulate how we feel emotionally, without causing harm to others or our self is seldom learned and is not an easy trait to attain. Often, the biggest mistakes we make are those that occur via emotionally driven rage.

The internal opposition of logic and emotion can lead us down many rabbit holes. In the coming of conscious awareness, many questions arise and the thin line between awareness and madness becomes evident.

Pondering perspectives and challenging socially accepted ideas is a very good way to involuntarily repel acquaintances and isolate yourself, as much of society is unwilling to wonder of such things.

I am of the belief that good and evil exits in all humans (even the fancy ones that wear robes). Now, you could argue that all evil is based on emotion, be it greed, jealousy or hate and to some extent I would be inclined to agree with you. Though as you progress through these pages you will stumble upon my position on this.

If good and evil exists in all humans, this would suggest the idea of a metaphorical set of scales within the human mind, tipping more toward one way or the other, based on any given external stimulus.

In being aware of these scales, the psychological variation in humans reveals to us just how well some people have their faculties in check and just as importantly, how many do not.

Awareness reveals the vibrancy of the human mind in all of its glory. The sheer discipline that many have acquired to resist limbic impulses and equally, on the other side of the coin, reveals the feeble minds of society.

Human virtue provides us all with the awareness of what is good and what is bad, hence laws. The devil in all of us calls us to the void. Ominously suggesting impulsive ideas that seldom become physical reality.

Although evil is present in all of us, good is fortunately there to quash it and balance out the scales. This war is timeless and will forever exist. The opposition between good and bad, logic and emotion will forever be.

Those that reject this fact are under egotistical delusion. Ego is an intelligent fiend, the anti-hero that is behind human survival yet equally an arsehole.
Ego is an enigma that can be both impulsive yet calculated, strong but sensitive and fierce but yet so very fragile.

The internal war is in reality a love affair of what it simply is to be human and imperfect. We naturally, egotistically have an expectation of human perfection and divinity.

Though we are so very far from this. Personally, I have found modesty and comfort in the acceptance of the fact that I am part of nature, recycled energy that will forever be. There is a poetic beauty in this and that is enough for me.

Learning to separate your logical mind from your emotional mind when self-reflecting, will offer up some interesting internal conflict that is not easy to decipher, although it does allow us to understand the motivational foundations under the decisions we all make.

Understanding why someone has made a specific decision does not necessarily have to mean that you agree with it. Understanding behaviour is not the same as condoning it. It just means that you have had it in you to try and see it through their perspective. This will in turn make you an observer.

My own life is a complete paradox of sliding doors swirling in to Fibonacci. When you understand that life is of low entropy, it hits you hard and you realise the importance and significance of your own energy and the directions in which you choose to aim it in.

Time is the most valuable thing we thing we have and we would fair well to be wise with it. Long-term happiness cannot be built on weak foundations. Chasing the dragon of short-term highs is that of the mentally feeble.

If your life is focused primarily on material possessions, the pursuit of notoriety and being negative about others, time will one day catch up with you and provide you with a healthy dose of reality. At this point, it will likely be too late for you.

To be mentally centered, present at all times and deeply in tune with your sensory system is what it is to be a complete person. Satori enriches the soul. Nirvana exists only in the perception of the individual.
When actively observing the world around us, clarity is essential and it is important to first understand that the world can be a very sporadic and intense place.

The branches of madness are never to be fully understood. Just know at the base of things, that most bad situations occur out of untamed emotion and vacant logic.

This is where practices like meditation and mindfulness would come in handy and my hope is that some day, they are taken seriously in schools so that the generation of the future may move forward with a higher and more logical perspective than that of their predecessors.

Without emotion, logic is chaos. Without logic, emotion is chaos. The balance must be consistent.

We all inherently have mental opposition. Those that do not realise this can find themselves in a state of frustration based on their difficulty in making decisions.

For example, logic would suggest that a lower global population would be resourcefully beneficial for the human race as well as prolonging our existence, however emotion would dictate that human life is to be sustained regardless overpopulation and the negative repercussions that this would entail.

This is a stark and potent example, although the message remains the same. Humanities greatest task is navigating the maze of logic and emotion.
We must learn how to learn, adopt patience and adapt. If only every conscious human being alive today was able to differentiate between his or her own personal logic and emotional thought processes, we would be living in a very different world indeed. Using self-reflection in all moments where you find yourself needing to make a decision will overwhelm you with other options that you previously did not ponder.

The truth is, shit happens in life. Nothing will ever stop that and you have no control over it, as there are far too many variables for one person to control at any given time. The only thing that you can control is your reaction to what befalls you.

Your reaction is the only thing that can ultimately dictate the circumstances following any event that happens. Seizing control of your reaction is vital and self-reflection in that moment is what will present you with alternative options, from the only one you felt existed.

We already know that emotion can block logic and it is in these moments of intense, overwhelming emotion that your options can become obscured.

The first thing to realise is that time is all we have and no decision has to be made on the spot. No matter who is or what is forcing you to decide in the moment, you will have time to think.

This of course is not easy and of no small feet. This is why the world is in a far more troublesome state than what it needs to be. Poor decision-making.

To initiate the process of making a better decision you must first self-reflect. Tune in to yourself deeply and calm yourself. Clear the pathway of thought and seize power over yourself.

Divide logic and emotion and figure out which of the variables in the situation at hand are within your control. Whether the situation at hand ends badly or well doesn't matter. What matters is that you did all you truly could to attain the latter with a calm mind that has learnt to differentiate between a logical decision and an emotional one.

Enhancing yourself with the ability to self-reflect in any situation and to be able to manually alter your state of mind regardless of circumstance is the next step in evolution in my opinion. It is not easy, but when you attain an understanding of these fundamental principles you will realise that it is a form of true power.

In a world where so many have eyes but do not see, you must become the difference. Others will follow and the world over time will progressively get better.

Seeing things from a higher perspective is a conscious decision to be made. Often a task that is dismissed as overwhelming emotions sink in, but developing the ability to do so will only bring better understanding of how to deal with the most intense of situations.

Decision paralysis occurs when simplified thinking is halted. We make things more complex than what they need to be. We become overwhelmed with our own thoughts. Yet they hold no physical reality. These barriers are self-imposed intangibles.

Meditate, exercise and set goals. Try to avoid the extreme excess of everything and apply discipline in your life. There will always be those that are skeptical and critical. Prove them wrong, not for their benefit, but for yours.

The various arguments ongoing in the world, when viewed through the grounded mind will be seen as pointless and that of the unevolved. All instances where countries and people argue over such parochial things and violence takes place, to me is evidence that we are not as evolved as we believe we are.

In the words of Crocodile Dundee *"You see the rocks over there? They've been here for millions of years, they were here before us and will be here long after us. Arguing over who owns the land is like two fleas on the back of a dog, arguing over who owns the dog"*.

Life is just a matter of perspective. Technology is not holding back, the arrow of time is moving forward and history has shown us that those not willing to adapt will fall behind. In this instance, keeping an open mind and a positive attitude towards learning will be one of the most progressive steps you can take.

They say that nobody really wins a war. I personally think that this is because war never ends. The war continues. It is just the players that change as the shift of power moves.

The comparative of world problems to that of our own on a micro level is stark.

We can only seize power of our own problems by becoming mentally equipped to do so. Every day I see situations taking an unnecessary direction, based on an unrequired emotional investment from either one or all parties involved in a situation.

Or sometimes when you're on your own, over-thinking. Causing yourself great anxiety based on things that only exist within your own mind.

Being a deep thinker has its positives and negatives. You learn that you are both your own best friend and worst enemy. Taming your demons can be made easier by pondering perspective variations. The issue with being a deep thinker is the abundance of perspective available. Like trying to dig your self out of a hole, only to become deeper in thought.

Navigating yourself out of troubled waters can be a long, laborious endeavour. Lessons will be learned and the arrow of time constant. The relief usually comes when you suddenly realise that 99% of the problem only exists within your mind and has no external reality. Understand that your emotions were trying to hijack your path of logic.

Instinct should always be trusted. The energy you feel is not your mind playing tricks on you. It's an internal sensory overload and a warning signal that has took millennia of evolution to develop. It is a survival mechanism that warns you of danger. Never ignore it.

Chapter Five

Mindfulness

The pursuit of finding meaning in life can lead many down a very dark path. Humans are not perfect by creation and staying on a good path can be a laborious maintenance job. Meaning itself is the goal, as without it many would fall in to boredom and depression.

The true enemy is not an individual nor group, it is the untamed animal that lives within us all. With that being said if we start with ourselves, and our own personal projections, then we as a collective can improve our lives and in turn everyday social situations can only improve.

I have come to the conclusion that life is just a matter of perspective and how you choose to live your life is dependent on how you see things around you. Your perspective is based on your opinions and your opinions are formed based on your experiences in life.

Whether they are bad or good experiences can dictate the kind of person you are. Understanding that our sense of reality is shaped by our experiences can hold the key to helping you make necessary changes that will undoubtedly improve your life.

Everything you do is a choice so therefore happiness is a choice. The hardest thing to do is have an open mind, always. Allow your mind to be an open conduit for information and do not be afraid to listen to the opinions of others, even if they conflict with your own. You may learn something or see something you believed from a different perspective that ultimately adds to your own.

We all get what I like to call "mind junk". Where our minds feel overwhelmed and full of shit, but this is just temporary and it is completely within your power to change the state of your mind. As humans we question everything and we can become engulfed with our own thoughts. This is where you need to change your surroundings.

Your body needs to move, you need to spend energy and not allow yourself to become stagnant. Your body knows what it needs to do in order to make you feel better; you just need to provide the opportunity for it to do so. The enigma of the human mind is so complex that we can only begin do understand it. We are corrupt yet we hold moral values, we are lazy yet spontaneous and we are stubborn yet empathetic. The mind is so sporadic yet we do yield some control over it.

I often wish that I wasn't such a deep thinker. It can lead you in to some troubled waters and negotiating yourself out of them can be a hard task. But keeping in mind that your thoughts are not reality tends to help. The constant sway from the past to the future can lead to some uncomfortable emotions and having the power to realise when you are doing so can be your salvation.

The only control you have is of the present moment and in knowing this, you can alter your state of mind. The past has already happened and the future is not yet here, so try not to fog your mind with intangibles.

It is a crazy thought that we ourselves are our own biggest enemies. We can see this on a day-to-day basis when we hear our friends or family being self-critical. This deep-rooted mindset is innate in us all and needs to be checked from time to time. We are creatures of habit and we must try to create a more positive mindset, especially in regard to ourselves.

The spectrum of contentment based on materialism can lure us in to a false sense of fulfillment and convince us that we are satisfied but ultimately, if this feeling of contentment is based on the material things that life has to offer, then how long will this contentment last, for as long as it takes for boredom to sink in? As is life, all emotions, including happiness are a maintenance job.

I truly believe that we are all here to help each other and this is where we can find genuine, long-term fulfillment in life. We all have that need and want for more, it is where we apply that need that defines us. This is evident in the rich always seeking more but blind to what more there is other than materialistic gain. The lines between the material world and the moral world become obscured by a lifetime of greed and self-indulgence.

Science has shown that all energy is never lost and that it can only ever be transferred.
Science has also shown that human beings vibrate on a particular frequency. We project energy in to the world. With this in mind, if we all made a genuine effort to take a moment to calm our negative energy and convert it to a positive, and projected that in to the world, wouldn't that make the world a better place? Or have I lost you?

Happiness is a choice and is completely based on the decisions that you make in life. We become our environments and our circumstances are dependent on our ability to be able to think in a given moment. Whether we react emotionally, which is usually by default, or have the discipline to remain calm and to think rationally, will always dictate the variables of an outcome.

Epictetus said that it is impossible for a man to learn that what he thinks he already knows. Pondering this, how much do any of us really know? Doesn't this open the door of discovery for us all? If so, that is some exciting shit we all have ahead of us if we can open our minds to the prospect of it.

No one human is here forever, but for only a short time. How much money, power and possessions does one person need before they realise that there is no real value in these things and that they cannot take material things with them after death? Only a memory will live on after death and be it a good or bad memory is what should be the focus of life. We live in a world where society is waking up to the idea of mindfulness, self-expression and awareness of how the world is being managed.

To be mindful is to be present in any given moment, aware of the ambient energy being emitted not only by those around you, but by yourself too.
By learning to interpret the wind, you can manipulate the sails to dictate direction.

In any given moment your mind is involuntarily aware of ambient detail. Your senses, gifted to you by Mother Nature to interpret your surroundings, grace you with the vibrancy of life.

A beautiful gift, to which if given full attention to, can provide an overwhelming sense of peace and fulfillment. Leonardo Da Vinci once said that everywhere you look in life, there is something to see, something to learn and that we will run out of time before we run out of things to see and learn. Or something along those lines…

The sheer depth of beauty in our world is staggering, though sadly, many have eyes, but do not see. The pollution of modern day conveniences and indulgences has reduced mankind's ability to interpret the world around us to a deaf, dumb and blind faculty of awareness.

Tourists with their open minds, absorbing the world around them like stomata ready to absorb the light. A lot can be learned from tourists. Use the tourist method!

I innately observe everything around me, including people. Not judging, but simply observing. I come to feel as though many are heteronomous; as though they are simple computers following a set of instructions obliviously, like an android or automaton. As though the brain has a virus, blocking its ability to absorb its surroundings.

The monotony of life overloading the emotions in a negative fashion, blocking the way of consciousness and the path for the sensory system to recharge and to feel at one with the natural world. Such is life that things are loved and people are used. I often wonder if this is all relative, or we are led to believe that it is.

I don't want to just give you answers that I feel are right, I want to plant seeds in your mind that blossom in to your own answers.

I remember seeing a video of a colour-blind man, receiving a gift from his family of a pair of glasses that would allow him to see in the same colour spectrum as non-colour blind people. His reaction took my breath away. He cried, his hand immediately covered his mouth and he inhaled deeply and embraced his family as the tears of joy fell.

Immediately, I wondered if the people of this generation and of this world would have the same reaction to life and the natural world if they learned how to be mindful. This is not me preaching, this is not me being "spiritual". This is my interpretation of how we as humans can feel inner peace and contentment.

When I was younger, my Mother had a friend. She was an elderly lady named Daisy. She must have been in her mid eighties. I was energetic, fast paced and an excitable seven year old.

Daisy was of a calm and patient disposition. She was wise and kind. I remember her asking me to sit next to her and although I cannot remember her words verbatim, I do remember that she told me about cars on a motorway, the cars in the fast lane, going so fast that they cannot see much of what they drive past.

All of the beautiful trees, flowers and animals. Then she told me about the cars in the slower lane, they were able to see and appreciate everything that they drove past. They were able to see every detail. She told me that it is best to be the car in the slow lane because you see more of life.

At the time, I thought I was being told off. But now, I realise that she was teaching me a life lesson. Many of us in this generation live life in that fast lane, unable to appreciate the details of life. We race through life and wonder why we live in a generation of anxiety-ridden millennials.

To be mindful is to live in that slow lane. Inevitably, shit will come your way in life. You have no control over this as it is relative to life. What you do have control over is your reaction to said shit.

By surrounding ourselves with conveniences we are day in and day out distracted from contemplating who we are. We have no time to think and to get to know ourselves. So much so that this temporary lockdown has people losing their minds in panic as they 'have nothing to do'. A sad truth, we have lost ourselves from our true meaning. By not taking the time for self-reflection we have become emotionally reactive rather than logically equipped to deal with situations.

I have memories of speaking with a man named Don who was of another time. He was born in the 1920s and had seen the world change through eyes that many living today have not. The conversations I used to have with this great man always enriched my life and widened my perception of time and meaning.

I remember asking him what life was like before all of the technology we have now. He said, "People just got on with it. People appreciated each other. There was always something that needed doing."

From this, I came to the conclusion that people find meaning in routine. It is when routine is challenged or lost that problems occur. This being said, it is through our ability to adapt in challenging times that will determine the state of the human psyche.

The quote 'Only the strong survive' very much plays in to the current global situation. However not in regard to the mortality rate based on the actual virus, but by those at home, willing to find means other than social media to keep themselves busy.

Those willing to adapt and develop new habits that before seemed laborious. How many unread books do you have in your house? They are not merely shelf decorations, but a means of learning and expanding the mind.

When was the last time you planted seeds in your garden, or cut your grass? This allows for headspace, meditation and gives off a sense of fulfillment. It emotionally enriches your life and fortifies your mind against negative thought. Gardening was one of Don's favourite things, even in his old age.

When was the last time you sat down and asked a loved one how they are feeling and actually listened to what they have to say?

There is so much we can do to keep ourselves busy. I mentioned earlier that humans are 'learning machines' and in this we can use the time we have to absorb information, not the useless kind from toxic platforms, but the kind that enriches our lives. Learn a language, learn how to cook a specific dish, learn how to do that thing you said you could never do.

Start to think more about your life. Think about the path you have been on and if it really is making you happy or just making you miserable inside. You have, and always have had the power to change everything. The only thing that has stopped you is yourself. Banish the excuses and develop a plan to achieve your goals.

Rather than being emotionally reactive, learn to be logically active. Clarity of thought is that of a champion's mindset.

Your reactions to any given situation are the decisive factor for your future circumstances. You are a product of your own choices. Your mind is the most powerful tool that you have. If you can learn to be mindful, calm, aware and present at all times, you will inevitably optimize your future circumstances and dramatically improve your wellbeing.

Go and fucking meditate… Meditation is not segregated to religion. Including a good fifteen minutes of quiet in your daily routine should be essential. Learning to disconnect from the digital world temporarily offers perspective on the realities of life. Eckhart Tolle once wrote: Thought requires consciousness, but consciousness does not require thought.

Allow for that to sink in.

Feeling calm and content in any given moment allows for the conduit of ambient absorption to open up. Freeing you of the constraints of surfing back and forward through the imaginary realm of time that the mind creates.

Of course, time itself is linear and certainly not an illusion. Often confused with consciousness, the simultaneous moment of our reality and the only true window of time that we have any control over.

This present moment when focused on, instantly dissolves any feeling of worry, anxiety or depression. For these feelings are only present when the mind wonders in to the past or to the future.

For example, how do you feel when you walk through your local woodland? Better yet, ask yourself why we choose to go for walks in nature. The answer is because the natural world provides sensory overload.

When walking through these areas, we become conscious of our breathing, the beat of our heart and we are completely present in the moment. Our stresses fizzle out and we feel better for it. We are emotionally recharged.

I feel the monotony of day-to-day life has created a web of emotional spaghetti in the human mind that has crippled our ability to remain present. Thus allowing for the onset of mental health variables.

Life itself is a maintenance job. It is important to spend time with nature, where you belong.

Mindfulness enriches life. Being mindful of others in the form of acceptance provides much peace of mind and calm enlightenment that enriches the beauty of the world through the eyes of the freethinker. The counter to this is a rife problem in society.

Why is it in some cases, that because someone is different to us, we have to ridicule and annihilate them? Surely this is not the same species of people that put a man on the moon, that creates beautiful art, that creates languages, culture and love.

Many examples of narrow-minded projections of hate come to mind but some stand out more than others. How dull life must be for those that fill their mind with hate. Why is it, when the life of an individual becomes somewhat monotonous, we often see negative radical behavioural changes?

Perhaps lack of meaning in life, results in a desperate attempt at finding any form of meaning, be it good or bad. I suppose this would depend on the mindset of the individual. Be them of intelligence and determined, or shortsighted and dim.

The sheer lack of discipline amongst people is the key factor in most misfortunes. Life is and always has been, a do-it-yourself job. You have those that lead, and those that follow, those that create, and those that will forever remain stagnant.

Blaming the world for their misfortunes, and by the very behavioural traits that got them in to their predicament, are unable to see that they have always had the ability to make the necessary changes to better their lives.

It is the default mindset you see, to which modern day humans have become accustomed. We aren't as busy as we once were due the conveniences of modern day life. We witness mundane, low-grade behaviours of hate, manifested originally by preceding paternal figures. Likely again influenced by some form of media propaganda to divide the masses.

No one, is born hating another, this behaviour is implemented. There are many examples of this behaviour, though these pages were not created to list them all.

Everything written so far, although varying in example, all orbits around the same projections and ways of thinking. There are endless examples that orbit around human beings emotional and logical projections that demonstrate our faults and also our accomplishments via the chain of thought explained. However, I would like to put an emphasis on self-reflection.

Self-reflection could be the catalyst that changes the world. Usually used under the umbrella of many religions, it is time to stumble upon the realisation that we as a species can use self-reflection without tying ourselves to any religion. It can be used as a vital tool for clarity of mind and decision-making.

An internal awakening is brewing and the moment you tune in to reality and find yourself in the stillness of the present moment, you will see things through a perspective that was always there but was never realised.

Like seeing colour for the first time you will be overwhelmed by the beauty that is our world.

Again, this is no easy feet but it is achievable. Recalibrating your mind, toning down ego and tuning your senses in to the real world, the one that is far bigger than the one in our minds is a good start. We have so much, but what do we truly need?

We are sentient beings. It is in our nature to feel and I believe actively working on our self will be the catalyst of long-term change. Clarity of mind can be achieved on a daily basis through applying structure to your life choices. Getting to know yourself on a deep level is key to understanding how to construct mental guidelines that lead to enlightenment.

The circumstances of your situation, no matter how dire they seem, do not define you and are by no means "just the way it is". You have complete power to change everything. The only roadblock is willpower. Once you have the will to do so, you may have to learn some shit in order to put a plan together and create a blueprint. The result of said graft will outweigh the effort required to achieve it. Your life will change.

Knowledge truly is power. "Nothing is given in life" is true in a materialistic sense, however life itself is given, and is the most precious gift we have. What is to be earned is the ability to appreciate the wonders that life offers us. Once you learn how to do that, you truly will see with the eyes Mother Nature has given you.

I find myself on a rock of hope for the future. I understand that my ideals are not the ideals of everyone else, although I would argue that most would like to see some changes in our world. You see, it is my belief that humanity, in its pursuit of perceived progression has become detached from nature and therefore blinded to our true purpose in life and all of the conduits of genuine happiness have been blurred by the immense amount of convenience and the consistent need for more.

We have become less human by virtue yet we chase virtue in the form of rights and acceptance. We force acceptance down the throats of the masses and shame those that do not abide. This contradicts the free nature of human beings to think as an individual, thus hindering diversity in society and fading away the nuances of life. Although one may hold a specific view, this view is just what exists in their mind and can be changed over time if the right exposure and education was observed.

By forcing an opinion on someone, you are mentally attacking them, which in turn can lead to stressing the individual out thus causing an emotional reaction, which is not the conduit required for change.

I am not defending arseholes, I am just expressing that they have a right to be an arsehole if they so choose to be, so long as their view is not projected in to the world, who cares?

If one chooses to hold on to negative views, who do you think the one really suffering is? After all, you can only bring a horse to water, but you cannot make it drink.

You see, every human being holds a perspective on a subject matter. This perspective becomes an opinion, based on the information that is available. It is only when the information that was not available comes to light that opinions can change.

The danger comes when an opinion is believed to be fact based on conjecture, and the very concept of listening to the perspective of another is a no go. Like concrete, their opinions become solid when movement does not occur. We can see this in many different instances, many of which I have already written about. It's food for thought.

As an observer of humanity, I feel that our numbers have grown immensely in an incredibly short space of time. Many jobs have been taken over by automated machines. Social media has connected the world like never before and is a smelting pot for false news, fear mongering and the implementation of depression and anxieties. I have noticed that people are struggling to find meaning, so they find false meaning in things that were not issues in the first place.

Many people genuinely have nothing to do with their time. They are bored and unable to find positive purpose. This is a problem. Many have become so blindly tuned in to their emotions that they are blind to all logic. Every reaction is an emotional one. Gossiping, moaning and bitching until the cows come home. If one found true purpose and understood the realm of true happiness, they would not be talking shit about anyone else, why create such negative energy?

The pure life of understanding that everyone is going through their own troubles, which often the world does not see, can be used as a method of compassion. Why frown at someone when you can smile? Why create negative energy when you can create good energy?

These individuals are in dire need of an emotional detox. Getting outside is the first step. Not just any outside, but somewhere so overwhelmingly beautiful that it kicks them out of an emotional state and in to a sensory state. By tuning in to ones senses one can breathe, like really breathe, the thing that we do every second of every day and often forget that we are doing it. Feeling the air entering and leaving your lungs is the practice of many of the world's most peaceful minds.

We have become so caught up with a false pretense of life that we are blind to what life really is. Life is to be lived, life is to be absorbed and appreciated. We are the lucky ones that are here, for a short while no less, which in turn reinforces the importance of absorbing everything that life has to offer.

Experience as much as you can, live and breathe life as though you are reborn every day. Do not adhere to the standards of others, create and adhere to your own. It is important to stop separating yourself from nature and to realise that you are part of it.

Over the years I have observed many people absorbed in a self-manifested chaos that brings no joy. Making peace with enemies is liberating. It frees you of the self-implemented negativity that was clouding your life. Free yourself and let go of your ego. Life is short and time waits for no one. It is only you that blocks your path to happiness.

You have been gifted an advanced brain and an advanced place in this animal kingdom. Seize control of your mind and realise that most things that trouble you are well within your control to change. It is all based on your perception of things, how you translate things within your own mind.

Whether you translate a situation logically or emotionally, weigh up the outcome and think long-term to what is best for you. Have you ever noticed how your silence is noticed more so than your words? If you allow yourself to not become emotionally invested in the bullshit life likes to throw at us sometimes, then you have reached a heightened state of mental and self-awareness.

This is a win for you that can never be taken away. Always take that high road and look after your own mental state by gifting yourself the moment to think freely in any instance. I am no angel in this sense. I have been in many situations over the years that I could have dealt with so much better than I chose too. But as said previously, life is a maintenance job and shit happens sometimes. It is the pursuit to always endeavour to do better that counts.

Sometimes we fall and show our hand to the arseholes in life, whether this be a build up of frustration or an impulsive moment, we must always try to do and be better. Life is but a bunch of lessons that we try to learn and pass on, therefore mistakes are allowed and an essential part of being human.

Things happen sometimes that require a call to action. We are not in control of the minds of others and when the fight comes to you, you have to be ready to fight back. This is a sad truth in the physical sense. In the mental sense, being prepared is a powerful tool. Prepare your mind to be ready for anything.

This is not to say that you should adopt a sense of false confidence, it is to say that you should make yourself deeply aware that life will often throw some unforeseen scenarios your way and that you should expect it from time to time and be mentally prepared for when unexpected situations happen.

Our lives are not in the hands of some form of malignant fate, but in our own hands. You are not you until you learn to control the minds that live within your own head. Your emotional mind will torment you, tease you and trick you in to believing things that haven't even happened. Seizing control by remaining centered and in the present moment and only focusing on what is within your control is when you will find peace and the logical mind will prevail. Making a logical decision to not become emotionally invested in things where it isn't necessary will bring an abundance of peace to your life.

Of course life is diverse, the nuances of opinion will always exist. Evil will always exist and so will peace. There will always be good people and there will always be bad people, this is nature.

All we can do is strive to be the very best person we can be as an individual, we must focus on our own little bubble and project as much happiness as we can in to the world.

Of course, shit will come your way from time to time. Address it, let go of it and move on, endeavour to not energise that, which does not bring happiness to your life.

Learn to let go and understand that the key to life is that you are never actually in control. The constant maintenance job of managing our own emotions is laborious, but worth it. Finding peace is no easy feat but once tasted, it will become the pursuit of a lifetime.

Every day that you wake up is a blessing, with the abilities to interpret everything around you and to interact with things as you so please. This is the vibrancy of life. You have a choice, you can independently choose how the manner in which you interact with everyone and everything. The energy in which you choose to project will dictate the narrative of your life. With this logic, be tactical with what you project as the energy you receive back will mirror it.

Chapter Six

Social Media

The minds of the past were unfiltered, active and free. They pondered consciousness and questioned everything. Undisturbed and undistracted by the excesses of eccentric and indulgent conveniences that we now possess, their literature offering an abrupt lesson in freedom of thought, sentient and attentive to the physical world and able to beautifully articulate their thoughts and theories.

I enjoy technology, but I also see that see that it has filled the void of meaning in many. If social media were to be deleted, how many would lose their mind and sense of purpose and status, what would be left? Shrödinger's cat ever present in this paradox.

The cyber world creates a false sense of being to which fills the cracks of a lacking personality in many. Nature has gifted us fives senses in order to absorb the world around us, what have we become and what are we becoming?

Earlier on I wrote about ego. Social media is the microphone for ego in all forms. It has become a playground for cynicism. It plays in to who we are as beings and feeds the ancient tribal need for approval that has found its way to be lodged within our DNA.

We opportunistically show the vibrant, colourful moments and highlights of our lives, but what of the grey areas, those areas where in the furnace of the adaptable we build the foundations of our vibrant moments. Ambient expectation infects the mind like a virus.

To maintain a healthy mind, the one thing that you shouldn't do, are things for the approval of others. Humans innately seek acceptance and a sense of belonging. Today, the pursuit of this fulfillment is misguided.

Seeking the approval of others in the cyber world, from people you have never met and likely never will meet, competing with others for higher online social status, all via intangibles of zeros and ones. Who are you in real life? What are your real moral values? What do your closest people think of you?

Happiness may come from stimulus, but contentment does not. Do things for you. Ridicule will never be far, but what is ridicule other than a projection of comparison?

Beneath the surface of social media we are human and are surrounded by human problems, it is just that some like to pretend that they are not as it is a long fall from such a high horse.

Acceptance, validation and attention are what we hope to gain through posting snapshots of our lives. The means in which we fulfill this need has been enhanced to feed the addiction of the user to a point where most will only share content that has been highly edited and will only show false circumstances in order to maximize social approval and validation to satisfy our desires. Queue the partners of social media influencers and models and have the ring lights at the ready...

By default, your mind may reject a lot of what I am writing. But this plays in to my point. We have become emotionally dominant creatures so much so, that any concept of thinking differently is snubbed.

In the days of disposable cameras, we of course still took photos of special moments that we wanted to capture as a tangible memory, to be brought out years later to show to your son's new girlfriend. Thanks Mum.

These days, a false reality is fabricated and projected in to the world for all to see. Like by like and follow-by-follow our ego grows and grows. We live in a digital society of highlight reels to which comparison is rampant and all of the emotions that a green eyed, envious monster can muster are funneled in to a sense of depression and lack of self worth.

Reality doesn't go away because we stop believing in it.

Social Media is a distraction of logical thought that appeases the limbic system. Rendering the user a slave to the parameters of social expectation.

As many people do, I naturally enjoy the sight of a beautiful woman. But what do these exaggerated ideals do to the mind of a young impressionable lady seeking social approval? How does it contradict or alter their potential in life?

Unrealistic expectation leads to a rocky road of insecurity. Scenarios like this, which there are many variables of, in my opinion are an explanation as to why we live in a society riddled with mental health issues.

The need for attention is rife and the means in which people go to in order to attain it knows no bounds.

Often even what appears to be the most sincere acts of charity are done so for the reaction rather than genuine intent. For example, a celebrity will donate a large sum of money to a charity, more so to boost public image rather than having any care for those that are in need.

This may come across harsh, but my point is to not take a stab at the genuine goodwill of the celebrities that do so, as the donation will help those in need regardless of the motive. My point is to highlight where the moral compass lies within all of us.

We have all heard the cliché term that most things are okay in moderation. Though in regard to social media humans have as expected, drained the lake to the point of no return.

Social media has ironically exposed a very ugly side to humanity. This pattern of behaviour is evident in other areas too, though I will get in to this later.

I am not condemning social media. I am highlighting a pattern of untamed behaviour that I feel has been, and is detrimental to mental health. Social media is a good thing, when used wisely.

As I explained in chapter one in regard to emotion, when we have an emotional attachment to something, we are highly reluctant to relieve ourselves of it, to the point where logic will not be acknowledged, even when self-sabotage becomes evident.

Humans are victims to their own convictions. Forever in need of entertainment, running from the stillness of the mind, whilst finding purpose in vices.

I once stumbled across a question; it asked if you would be willing to delete social media in order to have a healthy relationship. Would you? Don't say yes just for the sake of saying yes. Truly think about the question and the reasons behind your answer. If the answer truly is no, what does this say about your priorities and what you give value to in life?

Social media provides approval and disproval from others, most of which from people whom you do not know and will never meet. Yet the approval or opinion of your chosen person means less than the opinion of these strangers. By default, your mind is currently arguing this point out of emotional disproval. But what does your logic say when you muster up the ability to settle your emotions and think rationally?

I know I am being provocative. But the world did not come to be, by means of understanding that were free from conflict.

Self-sabotage is a blind assassin in our modern world and we are all victims to it in one way or another. Your ego feeds your projections and your projections lead others to feel low and in turn lead them to fill the lacking void of attention by any means.

Minute after minute and hour after hour, we impulsively check our phone. Checking in on the lives of other people. Accumulating shocking screen time and effectively engulfing ourselves in to a cyber reality whilst suspending true reality.

Sacrificing a real, tangible reality for a limited one that does not enrich your life is like pouring years of your life down the drain. Self-imposed social parameters strip away parts of your personality, until all you do is solely for the approval of the cyber-society.

Like a hamster on a wheel, an emotional slave to a false reality. Why do we choose to be slaves to our own vices?

I enjoy social media and the idea of it. My issue is not with the tool but with the mindset of the user. Perhaps I am sad to see what I interpret as the vibrancy of reality being neglected by my own species.

Deceiving ourselves on a daily basis in to a false sense of meaning, which in reality are merely recycled means of finite pleasure. A slave to pleasures, chasing the dragon as it were…

I suppose social media is realm in which people can build an identity, an identity in which they can dictate the perception of, more so than they could in the real world. You can portray yourself however you like online and hide away your imperfections and the cracks of your reality from society. The irony is that it is within those cracks that you find yourself.

We live in a world where being your self is a scary ordeal. Many project false a representation of themselves for the validation and approval of others, that is far from who they truly are. You cannot preserve entropy, as disorder is inevitable. Meaning, you will grow less fond of your false self over time at the expense of who you truly are.

Most people are followers. They follow how others dress, speak and live, creating a society of copies to which everyone acts as an original. Cloned originals. I am quite sure the demographic comes to mind. Anyone who does not follow suit is seen as odd.

Judgment is profound and you are the enabler. Your behaviour enriches the state of society. Narrow minded expectation of how one should look, act and hold faux-liberal views is seen as the standard in the modern day. Everyone jumps on a bandwagon and ensures that they post about it too, trend after trend, reinforcing a false state of purpose in life.

Thinking is difficult, that is why most people judge.

- Carl Jung

Our generation is one of spoiled technological fortune but yet we use these tools to judge and ridicule each other, suppressing our true selves. Constantly comparing ourselves to others, like a polite battle of who has the better life. In the modern day this tactical gambit of self-obsession is plain to see.

We live in an oversensitive and fragile society. Life has become easy and has made people soft. Everyone is obsessed with themselves, trapped in a society of comparison, triggering anxieties and heavily diluting any form of benevolent behaviour.

The pernicious effects of social media will in the long term have detrimental consequences to the faculties of the masses. Spending countless hours playing video games as social skills deteriorate. Like a distracted dog with a toy we neglect the world around us.

So spoiled by choice that true love becomes a myth and all that can be, is swiped away through the cyber world. Our reality becomes a cyber reality, a mentally toxic abyss that few can escape from. In a world of constant comparison we wonder why we have a world full of anxiety-ridden millennials.

The children of this generation are smothered with technology, poor nutrition and a huge lack of social intelligence.

I'm not suggesting that we must do away with technology. I am pro-technology. I am raising the

conceptual idea of realisation that the world is not limited to the screen of a smartphone and that we should ponder the idea of living in a moment rather than recording it. Absorb the energy and be free.
To each their own.

In a world that has never been so connected and informed, how can we use this resource for the betterment? How do we use it to it's full potential?
For every question that goes through my mind, I end up with more questions.

Imagine getting to 70 years old with the knowledge of how many hours that you have spent looking at a screen and not living in this beautiful world we have around us. Enjoying every moment as though it was our last. Fuck that. Life is a blessing and how we choose to spend it will define our happiness when our time comes.

On a personal level, through observation I am constantly reminded of the predicaments our generation faces. As life has become easier and more convenient, standards have risen but yet in a lot of cases, work ethic has not. I know many people that feel the world owes them something in a materialistic sense but yet seldom make any efforts to attain what they want.

I have met people that hardly have any money but yet for a social media post will pretend that they live a life of luxury, videoing themselves, falling casually out of a G-Wagon that doesn't belong to them to paint a false sense of reality for the world of social media. What has the world become?

Under the guise of social media the lines between reality and expectation have become blurred and as a byproduct, we face a pandemic of a generation plagued with expectation and disappointment. This has led to an abundance of depression and anxieties due to a false feeling of lack of fulfillment.

Whilst so many are busy searching for more, they neglect what was always in front of them. Happiness does not come from external things breathing happiness in to you, happiness comes from you altering your perspective on the things around you and paying attention to what is often missed or overlooked.

False expectations based on comparisons to others highlight reels is a very unhealthy way to lead your life. Everyone faces challenges; everyone struggles from time to time. No human is exempt from this. By nature, we are all critical of ourselves and when an opportunity arises to only show our best side, the majority will take it based on their need for approval.

Humans by nature, in most circumstances can be opportunistic and impulsive. The challenge is to learn how to be disciplined enough to control ones impulses. If you portray and image of yourself to the world which is false, are you lying to the world or are you lying to yourself? If it were the latter, perhaps some self-reflection wouldn't go a miss.

As there is no fairness in nature, life truly is what you make it. It is a harsh reality that many seldom realise.

The best approach is to find happiness and appreciation in the little things that are usually overlooked. This will help you to gauge real emotional expectations of life and to keep you in check.

Realise that your life is your own and the expectations you have should be tailored to your own goals. You have to find your niche in life and conjure up the belief and courage to pursue it. Regardless of doubt or doubters. We all feel doubt and we all have doubters.
Unfortunately my biggest critics are those closest to me, but yet I persevere.

This world is wild. Feelings are deep and emotions are high. When we dare to look outside of our bubble we are hit with so much chauvinistic behaviour that it can be difficult to focus on our own mission in life.

For me, that would be to have this book being published and finding itself in the hands of freethinkers, to marry the person I love and to travel this beautiful world with them. Our ideals are a personal vision and the ideals of two people are seldom the same. This is what makes the world such a diverse place.

A sad truth is that I know people that put so much of their self in to their platforms that it has become the only thing that they feel validates them. Recording every moderately interesting moment of their life in order to hand pick the best moments to show people they don't know. I can't help but ponder the idea of life without social media.

What if all of the power was to be turned off? What if the social media plug was pulled? Deleted over night and completely irretrievable. What effect would this have on the social media dependent community? How would the attention seekers survive? Who would feel as though they lost their meaning and purpose in life?

If social media perished, would those dependent on it also perish? I believe that there would be suicides and mental health would sky rocket. An interesting and heavily concerning thought to ponder.

All things are just things. They bear neither personality nor traits. They cannot be bad or good. What gives things traits and value is the result of human interaction with them.

Things bring out the good or bad in people and it is by this that we determine whether the thing is bad or not. Disregarding or ignorant to the perspective that it is indeed the human behaviour that is at fault, not the thing. Things either bring out the good in people or the bad. Unfortunately it is usually the latter.

People become their environments. The core of the issue we have is that our current environment is contradictory to sustainable happiness. The meaning of life is to find meaning, and different people find meaning in different things. Our environment tends to dictate our choices of meaning.

Many have found meaning in social media and like most human vices we have taken it to an extreme.

We live in a society of comparison, passive aggression and false morality.

People chase the dragon of social acceptance in order to feel that they belong, rather than being them self, truly and unapologetically which in turn would attract a circle that loves them for who they are and not the false projections we so often see. This is why we have a generation of anxiety ridden young people.

Social acceptance outweighs self-acceptance.

Chapter Seven

Mental Health

The pursuit of finding meaning in life has the potential to lead many down a very dark path. Humans are not perfect by creation and staying on a good path can be a laborious, maintenance job. To find meaning itself is the goal, as without it many would fall in to boredom and depression.

We are not perfect. Perfection is but a perspective of an individual, that when is shown through the eyes of the individual can be appreciated by the many.

We all make mistakes. Not one of us is walking around with a head of memories that they wish they could release. The arrow of time moves forward. There is nothing we can do about the past but learn from it and improve from our mistakes. Establish your moral values and never sink below them.

No matter how hard that you work on your flaws and no matter how much that you improve as a person, there will always be those that believe that you are your fuck-ups. You are not.

Many make judgments as though they themselves are angles. They are not. I have made many fuck-ups in life and I have learned many lessons along the way and I am the person I am because of them. I have hurt people, upset people and had a looming bad reputation.

But none of these things define who I am. What defines who I am, is in my ability to identify and learn from my mistakes and the manner in which I choose to conduct myself going forward. Admitting to yourself when you were wrong can be a difficult yield.

The chatter of the hyenas will always be constant. They will all tell you how well they know someone, whilst at the same time talking the utmost dog shit about them in their absence. Who does this say more about?

It is for you as an individual as an individual to make your own judgment on another, only when you have met them in person and felt their energy should the foundations of your view on that person be built. Conjecture-based assumptions that are built from the opinions of gossiping hyenas are no way to conduct your independence.

You become your peer group, losing your ability to think for yourself and to think freely should never be a sacrifice for assumed friendship. Based on their evident behaviour, the chances are that they are talking about you too in your absence.

By nature, men are simple creatures emotionally and this can be the bane of a woman's life. But take comfort in knowing that you have emotional superiority. No one is perfect by definition. Everyone fucks up from time to time, but it is in those fuckups that we learn to grow as people.

At the time, we all had our reasons, or at least in the moment we thought we did. Your mistakes do not define you. Although life is no fairytale, we have the ability to make it so. The choices that you make and the adversity that you overcome will inevitably shape the life that you live.

Happiness is a choice and requires hard work. The things that you worry about do not matter that much in the long term. A heavy mind always seeks solace in nature. Often, life isn't fair. When your world is shrouded in darkness, there will always be light on its way.

When you hit rock bottom, you have to say fuck it and endeavor to better yourself. Work on you and surround yourself with the things that you enjoy. All negative emotions are temporary, like passing clouds they will soon be gone and the sun will shine again.

There is a calming beauty in knowing that all of your troubles will pass. No matter how dark the tunnel there will inevitably be light, this is out of your control. Our emotions can cripple us but on the grander scale of things their rampage is short-lived.

The foundations of who you are and what you have will always remain. There is nothing more calming than observing nature. Watching the oceans waves, standing in the rain or laying under the stars.

Leading you to an overwhelming realisation that time stops for no one and that life is too short to spend worrying about things that have already happened or things that haven't. Your happiness outweighs your worries and your happiness is defined by your strength and will to fight for what you love and hold dear.

What you can take from your lowest moments are lessons of appreciation for the little things in life. You have been to the depths and in the process of rebuilding yourself; you have upgraded everything about yourself. You have learnt to rely on yourself and no matter what happens, you have your own back.

This in itself is a blessing. Even when others turn their back on you, you are not the one without. Be the person that has a lot to give, not the person that is always in need. The world will be lucky to have you.

Self-development is key. Meditation is not just for Monks and Hindus; it can change your life. Exercising often, getting a good nights sleep, self reflection, learning a new skill, drinking less, travelling more, appreciating friends and family members are a small list of things that can help you reconnect with your mind and improve your life dramatically.

It is only you that can change the status quo. In no way am I trying to talk down mental health troubles, I am offering an avenue of solution that I personally felt helped me get through some very dark times. In my view, being medicated for thoughts that are triggering off emotional trauma is not the answer if you are seeking long-term improvement and happiness.

The first thing is acceptance. It is perfectly normal to feel sad sometimes and to have off days. We all do, and it is part of who we are. None of us can function at 100% all of the time. But a weed must be pulled from the root.

The catalyst must be discovered and faced, dissected and broken down in to pieces that are less difficult to be processed mentally. As well as facing our problems head on rather than masking or avoiding them we must try to be in the constant mindset that life and time moves forward and stops for nobody.
We cannot feel angry or upset forever. Time will inevitably heal you. However there are certainly things you can do to speed up the process as stated above. Filling your life with what you enjoy and love to do will inevitably improve your long-term morale.

Send out that energy that is truly you in to the world and watch how naturally people will be drawn to you. Not just any people, but your people who truly love you just for being you.

I recently read a book on the origins of humanity and when I finished the book I had a lot of questions. One of which was in relation to modern day human mental health and that of our ancestors. This once again triggered off more questions (it's a curse).

Now, I was thinking about the idea of survival versus convenience. If you think of us as wild humans where the survival of not only ourselves but also our family and tribe is paramount. We would be spending all of our time outdoors, moving.

Building shelters for our family and our people as a community, hunting, digging up root vegetables, picking fruit and climbing trees, fishing and diving for food, chasing off threats and focusing on reproduction. Dancing around fires, making tribal art and tools. We would be very busy, very fit and have immense social and environmental intelligence.

I take this and I compare it to how we live in this modern day. I naturally think of a TV remote, a piece convenience to change the channel of a box that is two feet away from your tired worn-in sofa, ironically watching a nature documentary or other humans socialising on a tropical island.

Not having to worry about moving to eat as your phone has multiple applications to conveniently have you eating within the hour.

Bonds are maintained through social media and you have no need to go out to satisfy your natural needs as websites synthetically fulfill your fantasies. Depending on a swipe left or a swipe right to meet a potential life partner, rather than going out and being the intended social creature you was supposed to be. Highlight-reel applications triggering off social comparisons and a need to have what everyone else has.

Then we wonder why we have so much anxiety and mental health issues in the world that can be conveniently medicated. Interesting thought.

We are spoiled by time. We have so much time to ponder things that are genuinely irrelevant to our personal lives and we allow these things to corrupt our emotions and sense of wellbeing. We become so emotionally dominant that all sense of logic is lost. We have become weak and blind to the root of the problem.

Convenience is not a bad thing; it only becomes bad when the sense of moderation in all things is abused. Moderation in itself is the answer.

With these two comparisons, I have come to the conclusion that we have forgotten a lot about ourselves and become emotionally very weak and like Icarus, we are flying dangerously close to the sun. In the absence of moderation and self-reflection, we find ourselves dwelling over problems that lead to a very negative and unhealthy mindset. I would however argue that the recent resurgence in modern day culture of meditation and yoga has certainly shown that we are in some way aware of what we have forgotten.

Our attachment to the fruits of the modern world has left us in need of some true awakening. Like a lion that has forgotten to roar we have in many ways become shadows of our former selves. Putting your phone down and leaving the car keys at home is a decent idea when in need of some you time. Getting in touch with nature on a regular basis will give your soul the pressure release it has been craving. Why do you think going for walks in nature feels so good?

Someone once said that weeding is a maintenance job, even to the most tended to gardens. The same truth is with your mind. Emotions are innate in all of us and often need to be checked. The ease of life has led to laziness both physically and mentally. Things are designed for your pleasure, like a ball to a dog. We never know when to put it down, even when it is tiring us. By nature we are adaptable creatures, this plays in to both good and bad adaptations. It is paramount that we learn how to create a balanced mind.

In this modern world where we are all connected like never before, it is evident that many suffer with social anxieties. Until recently I believed that anxiety was just something we all felt from time to time and it was just another emotion that is innate in us all.

Therefore making it to some extent completely normal and that it should not be seen as a medical condition needed to be treated with pills. Human problems, I guess you could say.

To some extent, this is still my belief. I personally grew up in a hectic environment so perhaps I learned from a young age to manage my anxieties in the knowledge that the catalyst would pass over like a cloud in the sky. But as of late I had an experience that overwhelmed me.

Being someone that has made a conscious effort in life to break my negative emotions down in to smaller segments that I could try to understand and mange through thought has helped shape who I am as a man and to see logic in even the most intense of moments. Having this self-discipline has allowed me to overcome some true tests that life has thrown at me.

A while back, something happened that I had never experienced before. I had a panic attack. It overwhelmed me to such an extent that I was shaking.
All chain of thought was off the table and I was unable to produce any form of logic to save myself from what I was feeling.

I took my quivering self to the shower and made it as cold as it would allow in the hope that the cold shock to my body would somehow reboot me. I stood in it for about ten minutes attempting to understand why I was in this state until the point where I could no longer stand and I had to sit down. Taking deep breaths I completely lost control of my emotions.

As hints of thought began to voice reason I felt it would soon be over. I stood up and turned the shower off and went out to the balcony where my then partner was waiting for me. My male ego was reluctant to allow me to voice how I was feeling to her, as I did not want her to see me in a weak state.

She began to speak and I could feel my body beginning to shake again, I cut in as she was speaking. "Babe, I don't feel quite right". The words left my mouth impulsively. She immediately was attentive to me and asked what was wrong, I said that I'm not sure but I felt so much anxiety and I wasn't sure why.

She grabbed my hand and we began to talk about it. Initially I was reluctant as I didn't want her to absorb how I was feeling and I was used to being someone that was able to self-regulate my emotions.

We spoke about it for an hour or so and came to the conclusion that I had been side stepping a lot of what was going on in my life at the time and that it had completely caught me off guard. I had a lot going on in life and I had developed a build up of backlogged emotion.

So much emotion, that my logical mind was unable to keep up and that I was feeling things that were alien to me.

In hindsight I was caught off guard and in total disbelief, the border between logic and emotion was obscured. Not understanding how I felt built up internal confusion. Although this all seems quite positive and beautiful, emotion being good or bad, when unchecked can lead to chaos. It was an internal bump in the road that once I understood, I was able to get over and see all of the good.

The reason I told you that personal story, is to highlight the importance of talking about how you are feeling. When you allow something to bottle up it can cause a lot of damage that could have otherwise been avoided.

When speaking about how you are feeling mentally there is a fear that you will be judged and seen as weak. I understand this, but it is not the case. It takes a strong person to show their vulnerabilities to someone. The best medication is to open up about it, before it grows in to something that will engulf you and create greater problems. Never be scared to talk about how you feel. All we have is time.

The only true commodity and the most precious thing we have. If we could for one moment truly contemplate our short life span, I wonder if some people would spend their time more wisely. You would not invest large sums of money in pointless things, so why would you spend your most valuable asset on them?

With this in mind, will the pursuit of finding meaning be altered from pushing personal belief systems on to others or would it be re-directed in to helping others and building a beautiful life of peace and appreciation? I often ponder the agendas and priorities of others and wonder if they are even aware that they are alive.

I have seen people so absorbed in self-destruction that the concept of being better seems otherworldly to them. I understand that you can only bring a horse to water and that you cannot make it drink, but in this instance I wonder if some can even be bothered to make the walk in the first place.

Meaning, even if they could, would they? Or do they even want to? Human variation obviously allows for people to go through life like this and I accept that. But for me, it is one of the saddest things to see so much potential wasted.

We all have the ability to make choices and it is in those choices that define us. I have learned that some people just enjoy being an arsehole and I have come to the conclusion that it originates from their own insecurities that they impulsively feel the need to project in to the world.

I have watched egotistical men wind each other up constantly to test the other and see how far they can push them. If this is their only way of self-validation and they serve no other purpose in life but to cause emotional anarchy in society, at what point do they realise that they have spent the most valuable asset that they have on a life of meaningless actions?

Again, I am observing through a psychological standpoint. Based on research and pre-existing suspicions, I put this toxic behaviour down to lack of affection and proper care as a child. Leading to instinctive survival behaviours that unfortunately project negatively in to society. The problem started at a young age and has lead to a misdirection of brain development causing deep insecurities that fall in to emotional withdrawal at a later age.

They find themselves depending on routine and group loyalty. Being territorial and constantly challenging rivals. A completely dark realm where no logic can shine a light as the emotional brain remains shrouded in toxic smoke. The very concept of talking about their emotions is dismissed and run away from, as it is too dangerous for them to explore. Understanding this behaviour helps us understand a lot of historical occurrences and reasons why our societies have been shaped the way that they have been.

Actions are made through impulsive aggression, as it is the only way that they understand how to project what they are feeling. All feeding the ego and in effect, making the world a darker place. A lot of these guys have huge cortisol levels (the stress hormone). Some find relief in alcohol and drugs, others by directing their stress in to sport. Which I believe is a more positive approach, although losing can have extremely detrimental effects.

We are all victims to our ego and some a lot more so than others. Varying in reason, there are of course measures that can be put in to place in order to check our self. Ego is fragile, and it is in that fragility that we can find cracks in order to infiltrate it. First of all, self-reflection needs to be put in to place.

The ability to be able to accept that you can be critical about yourself and that you, like everyone else, are not perfect. We have all gone through shit. It's how we allow it to effect who we are as people that defines us and shows our true strength. Accepting what has happened to us in the past is no small feet but it cannot be scaled if you aren't willing to take the first step.

A moment of self-analysis can be the bridge between realising the error in your ways and becoming a better person. Treating others as ego-boosting cattle only reflects badly on you. Upon realising this, you will have a deep feeling of self-pity. Upon which you will either dismiss or reject, or if you are strong enough, you will accept it and be willing learn how to change your ways.

I am a male so therefore I understand the mechanics of this way of thinking quite naturally. I see how self-destructive it can be and the effects it has on not only oneself but also the world around us.

Once you have realised that your ways can be altered for the better it will be vital that you are aware of your trigger points. The guy who just walked in who is larger than you or better looking is not your natural enemy. In fact the chances are that he is a really nice person and that he is just going about his day.

At this point you should be friendly, and pay attention to the build-up catalyst that you inevitably want to trigger in order to test him. The moment you feel it, you should self-reflect. Maybe even say that you need to go to the bathroom so that you can have a moment to yourself so that you can break it down and ask yourself a few questions as to why you feel the need to mentally attack this person.

You see, your mind is your own. If you cannot exercise control over it, then you are the weak one. Not them. Once you had your moments of self-reflection and come to the realisation that what you thought that you disliked in this person, is in fact something that is a reflection of your own insecurities, you can learn to manage it.

I understand that this seems like a very hard thing to do and almost impossible for you to even comprehend, but the moment you have done so, you have already made changes in order to become a better person, which in turn makes you an admirable person. Like anything, the beginning is always the hardest. But little by little you will be able to find yourself, and this will be such a personal victory.

This is a maintenance job for us all. Nobody is perfect and running at 100% all of the time, which is okay. It is the willingness to continue as optimistic as you can that counts. There is no better feeling than when you realise that you can have liberation against your own insecurities. The key is to lower your own resistance to change. Becoming aware of your own projections to the world and the effect that they have not only on you but the world around you.

Consider for a second, if your circle were to be asked to describe you, would they describe you or the things that you do? Examining yourself in this way will be difficult but this self-exploration will inevitably lead to discoveries that you never realised could be made. What you think is wrong in your world, must start with yourself. It's the way that you see things that must change.

The arrow of time stops for no one and I cant express enough how imperative it is that you start to understand yourself before you come to your final days and realise how much time you have wasted. Nobody wants to leave this world full of regret.

Once you gain momentum you will only get better and the world around you will realise it. You will develop real friendships, where the relationship isn't based on what you like to flamboyantly project in order to gain acquaintances, based on your need to be seen as the man, but based on people wanting to actually spend time with the person that you have become. What could be more satisfying than that?

You can, to some extent use your ego to help yourself keep it in check, the same way that you speak to yourself in order to work something out. Have I lost you? By being aware of what you do that is toxic, you can see it as a competition against yourself to not act like an arsehole. Keeping the goal to be a better person in mind, you can utilise your ego itself to force yourself in to check. Let's call that healthy ego.

Differentiate between that and your ugly, unhealthy ego. If you can do this, the process will be easier as you become more aware of when you are becoming dark. It's easy for an outsider to say you just need to meditate and to some extent this holds a lot weight and can be extremely beneficial in getting in touch with your inner-self and promoting a deep understanding on how you actually feel. Again, getting to this point is difficult, as you have to face yourself, without hiding.

We have a lot of means of self-discovery at our disposal but again it's taking that first step that is the hardest part. You must always utilise self-reflection in these scenarios and figure out why you would resist them. Start with yourself always.

Ask yourself this; what is interesting about you? What can you have in common with others? We are social creatures by nature and no matter how strong or stubborn we think we are, we need others and social contact. The issue is that a lot of people have interests, but they don't actually have anything interesting about themselves.

You will likely notice a lot of traits that you have in order to press your toxic ego, such as things like; having to be the one that can drink the most, lifts the most, spends most money or speaks to most girls. All of these things scream insecurity. In your head you think this will make you feel like the man, but in actual fact the rest of the world looks at you as a joke.

Everything is in excess and it will be your downfall in the long term. You don't want to be the "he's okay in small doses guy".

This will lead to some very lonely times for you. The light in all of this darkness is that you have the power to realise it about yourself and make the necessary changes.

Endeavor to try and not to think about how impressed others will be, but by how impressed you will be with yourself based on your actions.

Epictetus said that: *No man is free who is not master of himself.* Let that sink in.
It shows that throughout history there have been men like you. Some who have failed and died in regret and some that changed, and who are remembered forever.

Just like training in the gym, when you start to see and feel changes, your motivation will soar. This by no means is a gentle awakening and you will of course have some bumps as you endeavor to walk this path. But once you reach a certain point, the light of your life will be shinning so brightly that all you will want to do is continue on your journey. Let go of the past and move forward.

Knowledge is true power, so seek to saturate your mind with it. The part of your brain that is involved with experiencing emotions is called the amygdala. It is responsible for your perception of anger, fear and sadness. It also controls aggression.

It helps to store memories of events and emotions allowing the individual to recognise simular events in the future. Armed with this knowledge you can understand that your responses to things are based on prior scenarios.

However, no two situations are the same and it is in this awareness that you can alter your response by trying to remember the emotional outcome of a previous situation. By holding on to previous emotions, it cripples us moving forward in life. Learning to let go is difficult, but well worth the effort, especially for your own mental health. Pain can give you understanding, and it is in that understanding that will yield fruit of change for you.

You must discover your own potential and realise that it is borderless. The whole time you have been hanging on to destructive emotions that have led you down a rough path when all you needed to do was learn how to let go so that you can feel real happiness and fulfillment. I truly hope that my words find someone that needs them and that they resonate with you and that life only improves for you.

Some are so content that they have lost all vibrancy in their lives. This is a difficult one to explain, but if you bear with me, I will do my best to do so. Like undoing a thousand knots, it is often difficult to know where to start.

Here, I am going to attempt to explain what at first may seem like a contradiction to previous words, though if you give me a chance and read until the end, we may be on the same side of the field.

I argue that many seek fulfillment in the materialistic and often come up short in terms of long-term feelings of contentment. However, this is one extreme. The other extreme is of those that have become so content that life has become very dull and the concept of change in any area is inconceivable.

Having the same car for ten years, the same clothes and the same routine. Having lost all vibrancy in life and finding themselves depressed and with the absence of meaning. Sometimes it is good to hit the refresh button. It is great to be content but being overly content can leave life feeling very dull and bland.

This can be a hard place to recover from and seeking change can bring on anxious thoughts, but know that life is for living and taking chances. The very fact that you have realised that change is needed, suggests that you have nothing to lose.

It's very easy to blame the world for your own inability to take action, but ultimately it comes down to what you choose to do and what you choose not to do. You have to be kind to yourself, as though you are taking care of another. We are born, we grow from parental care (in most cases) and then we are solely dependent on ourselves.

We wash ourselves, feed ourselves and nurse ourselves back to health when sick. Yet we are not mindful of the actual act of looking after ourselves.

Why are we not? And why don't we be? Imagine mindfully looking after yourself as though you were someone that you care about. Applying conscious decisions as to what is best for you. Not smoking, exercising more, being nice to yourself mentally and trying not to be negatively too critical.

Buying your self a new wardrobe of clothes or a car, a new haircut, taking yourself to the spa. Consciously and actively making an effort to look after your own wellbeing is the greatest example of self-respect one can have.

In doing so, watch you life and your state of mind improve. Happiness is self-manifested. The circumstances of your life are based on the choices that you make, in every direction.

Having the will power and discipline is dependent on your level of self-respect. If you wont pick yourself up, who will?

Understanding that you got yourself in to a predicament and that you can also get yourself out of it will offer some relief. It all starts with the little things. By applying discipline in getting off of your arse and doing what needs to be done and by building positive habits and in turn creates a momentum of positive action, you will fall in to a flow state.

This flow state will carry you through to creating a strong mindset. Your quality of life will improve dramatically. You will soon see that everything you have always wanted is well within your reach and has always been down to you applying yourself.

You cannot win a game of chess without making any forward moves. In creating this strong mindset, you will be less susceptible to the bullshit of life.

Everything will be taken in to your stride, armed with the ability to differentiate between what is within your control and what is not will alleviate you of many stresses that were not intended for you. You do not always have to follow the crowd. Your journey is your own and you have been gifted a mind that has an innate ability to think freely.

Understand and use this in every situation. Create your own opinions, rethink opinions that you already hold and decipher whether or not they are in fact your own opinions or if they are based on the opinions of another.

In doing this, we can begin to create a world where society is not so easily influenced by the implementation of divisive control.

Chapter Eight

Religion And God

Humans feel. From the music we listen to, the sights we see and the memories we make. Listening to a river flow, the ocean waves crash and the wind blow. We may not be able to understand or define our comprehension of this feeling, but we know intuitively that there is some form of magic that has occurred, and occurring still.

The natural order of things operates like intricate clockwork. The functionality of all things feels purposeful and designed.

Our interpretations of this wonder have formed many perspectives over millennia and to this day still do. Surely the human mind could not fathom a definitive conclusion to the origins of nature.

It would be audacious and frankly, quite ignorant to draw a collective conclusion to which all must adhere. Early on in this book, I spoke of Mother Nature gifting us with our senses, in order to personally interpret this beautiful world we live in as an individual.

Your senses to see, touch, smell, taste and hear are your gifted abilities to absorb the magic of the world around you by your own means as an individual. When I speak of being present, I mean to give your senses your full attention, deeply. Awaken your sensory awareness.

Your relationship with God is by your own interpretation. Though this is contradicted by that human trait to follow, be it by force or lack of awareness.

I believe in God. Which is of my own interpretation. I do not feel that religion is necessary for the belief in God; I believe the two are very separate indeed.

Religion is a collective belief system with rules written by men. Pressed through humanity paternally by the delusional blind and fearful.

No person of a collective religious belief interprets God by their own faculty. They interpret God by the way it has been installed in them to do so. The concept of anything different is unacceptable and in many cases, punishable. Collective religion is fear and ultimately, a very broad stroke.

Your liberation is in your ability to become aware, to think and feel for yourself. Most people, even when they think they are thinking, they are just playing mental re-runs of what someone else told them, over and over again.

This works, because it filled the void of understanding within the mind and was reinforced with fear. The dogma of all religion, if followed to verbatim, would be absurd. You feel God, the religion in which carried the belief system is outdated and humanity has outgrown it.

Many readers will react emotionally to this and they will reject every word and hate me for suggesting this perspective. What people don't like, they refuse to accept. Emotion blocks logic.

Though as I have made it evident in this book, we know what an emotional reaction is. My hope is that there are logical minds and freethinkers reading these words. The open mind is a progressive mind, the closed mind never moves forward and as nature has shown us, the most adaptable not only survive, but they prosper.

Just as we have different words for things in different languages, we also have different words for God. For me, when I say God, I mean Mother Nature, she who gave birth to all life.

I believe that religion started off as something honest and of genuine interpretation. Though religious teachings and specific beliefs are based on a limited and primitive understanding of the natural world, formed long ago before the modern day understanding we have of the natural world and order of things.

In my belief, science displays the existence of God. Not a man sitting on a throne in heaven judging us, but as an active energy source that is eternal and is in everything. This in itself is ethereal. This is beautiful.

God did not make man in his own image. Man made God in his.

I feel man corrupted the very idea of God for his own gain. Is this not evident within all religions? Everything is for the gain of man.

God is what one feels deeply, a connection to all things and the very essence of life and beauty that we have been fortunate enough to freely adore. God is the energy that flows through each and every one of us. That flows through every plant, animal and atom in the universe. It is only when one calms the mind and pays attention to their senses that they can truly appreciate the spectacle that is life and be forever seeking satori.

Religion however, a corrupt and fear mongering tool of control and contradiction that was manufactured by man. Perhaps originating from good intentions though unfortunately polluted by millennia of greed and cruel intentions. However if Thomas Hobbes were right in his theory of the nature of mankind, some would argue that religion is necessary for the betterment of humanity and its sinful ways. What better way to convince billions of people to behave than to overwhelm them with the fear of Hell? Interesting...

I do not hold the opinion that religion is necessary in order to have belief in God or a higher power, equally I do not believe that religion is required for the implementation of human virtue and altruism.

Humans feel the need to understand and find meaning, and in some cases, forgiveness.

Therefore I understand the appeal of religion, and with keeping in mind that religion has been taught and passed down in to new generations for millennia, it is understandable as to why so many people hold it so dear.

Religion was forced on to people as the sole and only understanding of nature, it filled that innately human void and need of understanding, by default the very idea of thinking differently was seen as blasphemy and punishable by death in some cases. The beautiful art of freethinking was demonised and mocked.

Fear ensued for generations and the vice grip of religion led the minds of the people down a path of fear and obedience. Religion is a given understanding of our origins and our purpose, from a time where knowledge was limited. What we understand now but what could not be explained then, fell under the rhetoric of religious dogma.

The various conduits of understanding in regard to the origins of life are that of perspective and the product of freedom of thought. God is a personal perspective of an individuals understanding of life and what one feels intuitively. Science proves the existence of my understanding of God, as science is the window of knowledge to the laws of nature.

Religion is divisive yet portrays itself as unifying. This very truth, cements my principles that God is supposed to be a personal understanding and not a collective understanding.
Religious wars are an ever-burning flame that will never be extinguished, as the concept of religion itself has been built on very sturdy, emotionally based foundations where belief is built on faith rather than fact.

We only have to look lightly around the world to see the divisions that religion has caused. How is it that something that claims to promote peace and love as a collective can cause so much violence? The issue is that religion has been imbedded in to humanity as the only way to understand God and nature, cancelling out the art of freethinking.

The natural comforts people seek and often find in religion are answers to questions humanity has been asking and seeking for generations.

Holy books that have been written, re-written and re-interpreted for millennia will be able to provide perceivable answers to those seeking them. The same way people have become obsessed with horoscopes; these words have a way of finding open ears.

The idea is to think for your self. Find your own meaning and understanding of the natural world around you. Tune in to your senses and understand that you are part of an energy system that has been here for billions of years.

"Half the time you think you're thinking, you're actually listening"
- Terence McKena

Helping others is ultimately the greatest fulfillment one can have and a strong contender for the purpose of life.

To absorb the diversity of life and to observe the flow of energy through a calm state of mind is the most humbling feeling one can achieve.

Newtonian Mechanics has given us the law of conservation of energy. For if science has shown us that energy is never lost and can only ever be transferred, this would indicate that all energy is omnipresent and connected.

Therefore we, and all life on Earth are all connected by one common source of energy. Perhaps the only true contender to bear the name of God is Mother Nature herself. A constant recycling of energy binds all life as one forever.

Yet for all the beauty in the world and avenues of connection to what some would deem as "God" are completely ignored and disregarded. Sheer ignorance will be the downfall of a generation.

Until mindfulness is taught to the same regard as science, mathematics and literacy, humanity will forever be held back from its true potential. The selfishness that is shown by the greedy will ultimately starve the future generations of the beauty that is life.

The more a person is emotionally connected to something, the less willing they are to give it up. Dare I say, collective religion falls in line with what I am trying to explain.

We are hardwired to live this way. It plays in to our weaknesses, our curiosities and need for answers. These false answers that are based on limited knowledge to questions asked long ago, have become deep beliefs. If we are to believe in any one religion we are then expected to put aside our understanding on the laws of nature.

For all of these religious books written and thought up by men, they all appear to be above the laws of nature that we now understand in the modern day.

Reiterating my point about the potency of an emotional connection to something, we have become victims to our own assumptions and blind to logic and evidence based thinking. Any form of critical thinking in regard to religion is seen as offensive and in some parts of the world, illegal. I find this ridiculous and a complete insult to the freedom of speech.

God is not any one religion. All religions are interpretations of periodic understandings of the laws of nature. With vast amounts of implemented corruptions for personal gain. What had started off, as something beautiful has become something sinister and ugly for the vices and personal gain of men.

Many cannot handle any critical input that challenges their opinions, as their opinions have already been cemented in their minds as fact. The inlet of logic is blocked and any challenge is seen as an attack. Emotion wins again.

I find that many topics in the modern day fall under this umbrella, with the biggest culprit being religion as I have previously expressed. It has become offensive to even discuss religion in a critical way.

Why have people become so defensive of that which they believe is fact based on faith? My observation has brought me to the opinion that where religion has become so deeply ingrained in people over millennia, emotion has been attached to it as a defensive mechanism.

This is observable in the never-ending religious wars all over the world to which many of these wars are between those of the same religion but of different interpretation. The plot thickens… You never see a scientist becoming angry and violent based on an individual questioning their theories.

Humanity project their ideals and expectations on life, rather than themselves, expecting it to fit their mould. Leading to questions of *why would God do this?* God did not do anything. You just have a problem with what conflicts with your ideals. Religion is an ideal that conflicts with reality.

Religion and God are two different things. Collective religion is not necessary for the belief in God. Mother Nature gifted us our senses in order to interpret the natural world around us, to make a personal perspective on the natural world and our place within it.
By this logic, there should be eight billion religions on planet earth and not three main religions.

Your interpretation of God and the world around you is unique to you. It is objective to you, but subjective to others. As they have their own interpretations. Religion is the creation of man. It was created out of fear and for control. Religion only serves man. It is a corrupt belief system that has been dreamt up by minds that lived long ago, that had a limited understanding of the natural world.

In English, I would describe religion as a "broad stroke" belief system that ignores the variables of human perspective. Science proves that all energy is never lost, that it can only ever be transferred. The energy in you was once used for something else.

This means that there is one omnipresent energy source, a spark of life. God is not judging you and God is not a mind. But this does not mean that you cannot communicate with God, as you are part of what God is.

You are part of the energy source as all living things are. By this logic, prayer makes sense in order to connect with the energy source to which all has and does belong to. All forms of personal prayer are an attempt to connect to our nature, to our source of life. There is an almost unexplainable logic to this. One that you feel deeply, but yet the words are difficult to articulate.

I believe that just because something can now be explained by science, it doesn't stop it from being a miracle. Mystery does not make a miracle. Although we did/do lean on God via the conduit of religion, for things that we couldn't explain during certain historical periods, we now understand these things by means of scientific backed evidence.

We can now explain why certain events occurred and call bullshit on things that evidently didn't occur. This does not mean that a definition of God doesn't exist, as by my belief, God is the spark of nature that breathes energy in to all things. Religion is a poor understanding of God from another time where people were not intellectually able to understand the confines of nature through a scientific and open mind.

People were led and overcome by fear on a daily basis as a survival mechanism. With this dominant emotion in play, it helps to understand where the term "God fearing" comes from and why all sworn to God, bow down to the apparent word of God, which is no more than the words of many greedy and attention seeking, ancient hippies.

I don't believe it is for anyone to oppress or dictate the beliefs of others. But on the same note, I do not believe it is okay for pious monotheistic people to press their collective belief systems on to people who do not have religion. But have God.

Chapter Nine

The Natural World, And Us

This beautiful world is a marvel. It is rich and vibrant, it holds sights that can take your breath away and its grace can be overwhelming to the point that a teardrop can appear from no where.

When Mother Nature adorned this rock she did so wanting to gift its inhabitants with abilities to interpret her work. These gifts are your senses.

I pray her work was not done in vain.

The omnipresent energy of our universe and all that we understand, a spark of life that is forever recycled from being to being. There is no art or wonder that is equal to the natural world.

Sad it is that our gifts are so very neglected by the finite vices of human creation.

We belong to nature, it does not belong to us and we should forever marvel in the glory of the staggering beauty that is our home.

Our short-term visions have corrupted the natural order of things to a point of self-endangerment. Material profits create blindness and ignorance. In a time where we are all blabbering on about the concern of global warming, we regrettably neglect to realise that this little blue planet will be just fine. It is us that and the generations ahead that are in grave danger if we do not change our ways. How selfish we must be to ignore the wellbeing of our future successors.

Nature will reclaim this world in one form or another. We can choose to live in harmony with nature, and truly prosper or we can continue on path of flawed self-adornment and meet an inevitable and premature end.

The irony of a species thought to be of higher intelligence, bringing itself to an end by illogical means.

We do not only live once as we wake up and live every single day. In truth, we die once and it is our honour to live a life enriching our soul with everything Mother Nature has embellished.

Many issues that occur in the natural world through human involvement are of a mindset that we can see in day-to-day life. Usually revolving around greed, vanity and overindulgence.

To give you an idea, in the 200,000 plus years that modern humankind has roamed this earth, civilization as we know it is roughly 6000 years old and the industrial revolution *the start of the modern world as we know it* started roughly 200 years ago. In that time we have learnt a lot, and come a long way.

Rightly so, we should all be proud. Our achievements are astonishing. Yet that human trait of taking more than we need has led us down an eerie path.

Now the time has come where we must learn to be less reliable on what is profitable and convenient and more engaged with what is necessary and sustainable, both for the natural world and for ourselves. We simply can no longer go on this way and assume everything will be okay for us.

We depend on other species, they are a vital part of a broad ecosystem that supports and regulates life on this planet. We are not the only ones here and we do not own this Earth. The neglect we have shown has cut deep within the natural world. We have created disruptions that will forever be a reminder of the fault in our ways.

The irony is that many of the culprits are leaders of large corporations that tend to try and give the impression that they care, though the accumulation of their wealth came at the expense of the planet, making them hypocrites. When you learn how to observe the world through your two minds, you will see the world through many different perspectives.

Through observing the world around us, we will actively come to a realisation on just how crippled society has become by greed. Not only the leaders of big corporations, but also the leaders of our world.

Imagine for a moment that the leaders of our world were all taken to the moon to observe our planet from such a great distance. All of them standing there, gazing at our planet like a beautiful, live work of art.

All of the visible energy we know contained, oscillating and glowing. What emotions would occur in the minds of our leaders I wonder?

Would the realisation of their shortsighted greedy ways sink in? Would it change them for the better? When they come back to Earth would there be a new global perspective on what is truly important?

I would like to think, that they would be in awe and utterly humbled by the sheer grace of this planet that we share and that they would want to do everything in their power to preserve and protect it. World leaders are of different generational moral values and ideals. In an ideal world, world leaders would be of a similar age and moral accord.

Wars that end countless lives, and cause so much pain and suffering, that can be avoided if the long-term perspective was understood and acted upon. Trillions of dollars spent on global arsenals.

If world peace were ever to occur, those trillions could be redirected in to sustainable resources, to curing world hunger, homelessness and education. We could provide water and a safe place to sleep for everyone on a global scale. Becoming smarter as a species and ultimately propelling us forward in terms of organic progression.

But this dusty old dream is that of the wishful thinking optimist, a sad truth. This is where logic does not prevail unfortunately. Our biggest threat is and always has been ourselves.

Humans have evolved in many ways. However, this consistent desire to fight one another on a global and political scale shows that we are still not quite the intelligent species that we believe we are.

In a world where global peace seems but only a dream, imagine a world where all countries freely communicated and shared knowledge without the decisions of bureaucratic apes getting in the way.

Imagine a world where the soul agenda was the betterment of humanity and the preservation of our home planet.

An interconnected global authority that's agenda is to openly share knowledge based on the realisation that we are all living on land that is part of one planet and that we all come from this one planet and that we will progress faster and better as one people.

The fruit of this endeavor could give way to breakthroughs in many fields such as infrastructure,

medicine, technology and space exploration. Allowing logic and common sense to prosper is the biggest challenge we face. Fear and greed have grinded our evolution to a dead slow progression.
Humans have always battled with each other over their differences.

Rather than just accepting that our variation of perspective is what creates those differences and can lead to a greater understanding of the world around us. It is in our nature to learn, however if the path of learning is blocked by emotion, we will become stagnant and regress. The very key to our progression is hidden within the acceptance of the nuances of diversity.

When people hear I am writing a book, I tend to get asked what it is about. I usually try to keep it short and simple by saying "It's a comparative of how our world has been shaped by the conflict between emotional projection and logical thought". In truth, I feel both are necessary and the key is to find a balance between the two and to maintain it. Good and bad comes from both.

As of January 2020 our current global population is estimated to be 7.8 billion. By the year 2100 our world population is expected to be in the region of 11.2 billion. This is a huge number of people. In order for us to cope, things must change.

We must clean up our planet and reduce carbon emissions, clean the oceans, convert to electronic vehicles, utilise solar panels on all buildings, endorse tidal energy, build gigantic wind farms, find sustainable food sources and endorse companies that spear head the development of these agendas.

Of course these energy mediums are renewable, which as we know, the leaders of big corporations will likely try to block with their political influences. Greed wins again.

At what point do the masses realise that the world could be a Utopia if it wasn't for the greed of a few? It's not a complicated process to create a sustainable world.

We have the technology. What we need is a very large pair of scissors to cut through the ugly beast of red tape, fueled by greed.

Water and education should be deemed a human right and globally accessible. At minimum, this is what should be done on a global scale. Like squabbling children our elected officials are shortsighted in their global agendas. We have the potential to be an incredible species, more so than we already are. What will it take?

Throughout history and still to this day, the world's greatest minds are put to work to develop sciences for the agendas of the most ignorant. We have the ability to create technologies that supersede anything we have seen before.

With the awareness that intelligence and common sense differ, I couldn't help but to question what the hell was going on in the world and who was leading the circus.

We create nuclear weapons, which is a sin against humanity in my opinion. Why would we do this? Politics was made to avoid warfare yet governments spend trillions on "national defense" because certain individuals are blinded by greed and fear.

We as a species have the capability to make our world completely clean, fresh and emission free. We have the capability to literally power our planet in a way that causes zero environmental harm.

As a side note, it is important to know that when I say environmental harm, I mean mass self-harm. We need the planet yet the planet does not need us. We must remember this whilst on our high horses.

A brief historical financial burden is all that is necessary to increase the longevity of our species, to make the air we breathe clean and the water we drink pure. If not for us, then for our children and the future generations that will inherit any mess that we leave behind.

Taking responsibility as a collective is what is necessary. The Earths atmosphere and The Earths oceans are filled with green house waste and non-biodegradable spew that annihilates the eco system that we depend on.
Like a fat over-fed milk cow ready to topple over.

It is time to put this fat cow on a diet and get it back to health. I think we can do this and the world is certainly moving in this direction. We use fossil fuels as a dominant medium to heat water in order to create steam; this steam powers a turbine thus creating electricity, which is then used to power countries.
We burn illogical mediums such as oil and coal just to heat water. They serve no other purpose. There is an incredibly vast amount of money in the use of these mediums based on global demand for energy, which is obviously why we still use them rather than using a sustainable medium.

Like an ignorant snake eating its own tail. The truth is, we give money significance. We have far more mediums to use that are easily accessible and cause no harm. The issue is convincing those in power that there are far more important things in this world than money. It is like being stranded at sea and using slats of the boat as firewood as an eventual doom is pending based on our own ignorance.

We need only a means of spinning a turbine to create energy. The gravitational pull between the Earth and the Moon creates oceanic waves and crosswinds on this planet that we can also take advantage of and harness in the form of tidal and wind power. Completely economical and every country should be doing this.

These forms of power generation could change the lives of many living in poverty-ridden countries. We also have a ginormous thermo-nuclear reactor that lives in the sky called the sun that likes to come up every day emitting energy that we can harness, absorb and store.

Solar energy should have been utilised to its full potential decades ago. If a whole country such as Iceland can power itself on renewable energy, why can't the rest of the world?

There has also been much talk of seawater and the means of making it pure enough to consume. If we heat seawater to produce steam for energy production, how pure would the h2o be post cycle? I haven't found much research on this but the prospect excites me for the future.

One idea could be to collect the seawater condensate as this theoretically would be pure as the heavy impurities would be left behind which in turn, by using seawater for energy production we would also yield another useful byproduct in the form of salt, which is a 15 billion dollar industry.

All of these thoughts I often ponder curiously. It appears to me that there are some incredible ways that we can improve life in this world. I read in the news that many countries are aiming to lower their green house emissions by various dates in the future. Why not now?

The point of this book is not to waffle on about climate change or to protest about anything, it's purely an observation of human behavior that I can see is having detrimental consequences for everyone. I feel the global governmental application of science is failing us in a stunningly ignorant and subpar manner.

The planet itself is seeing some extraordinary changes for the better. It is healing.
Marine life is being restored all over the world and I feel humanity should pay attention to these humbling changes. We have become carried away with polluting the planet for financial gain so much so, that we are blinded and ignorant to the effects it has had.

The natural world is showing us stunning hints of its intent. We are seeing bioluminescent plankton glowing wave after wave, so beautiful and ethereal, it takes ones breath away as though staring in to fire. Hypnotised at the sheer beauty of the natural world. It is reminiscent of the Avatar movie.

Nature is returning to its intended form in such a short space of time, that it gives me hope that for all the damage being done, nature will forever win in its battle against the greed of humanity. We will forever be in sin as is who we are but an imperfect miracle.

It is evident in most people I meet or observe, their appreciation of the natural world and also hints of self-enlightenment. This fills me with happiness and restores my faith in humanity. In that moment, the natural world has brought them more happiness than any material thing they could buy.

A pure, unbounded and raw happiness that is un-measureable. Simple things, like appreciating a beautiful landscape, connections with animals, the apparent need to walk through the park for 'no reason'. This all calms the mind and creates a tranquil, logical pathway, the communication plane.
Listening, thinking and then responding is the hardest thing to do. Usually most just react with an impulsive

emotional response articulated in to words that tend to either make no sense or be an awful idea.

As creatures of adaptation we will always find a way. And as Darwin's theory of evolution suggests, the weaker of the species will die out, however not in our case. Subjectively, fortunate measures have been put in place to ensure the survival of the masses, regardless of ailment. Or for that matter, the sheer will to self survive has been shelved, as we rely on a convenient system of mass production to accommodate our endless needs.

Mass production of all things has squeezed nature dry, so much so that we have invented ways of speeding up growth, diminishing quality and contaminating food.

The natural order of things is at war with humanity's limbic system. Indulgence overwhelms us, making us lazy and expectant. We feel we are making ourselves happier, in truth we are blinded from reality. There is of course hope and society is in part paying attention to what is occurring before their eyes, and they are not happy. The question is what can they do about it?

As a consumer, you consume. The market will adjust to meet the demands of the consumer. If there is no demand for poor quality, mass-produced goods, then there will be no supply, as it will be wasting revenue.

Brace yourself for an unpopular opinion.
In my opinion, the very root of the issue is that global demand on resources is growing. The masses are medicated and immunised so less people are dying and global population is increasing. In 1960 the world population was estimated at just over 3 billion people and just 60 years later, we have more than doubled that number. That's a staggering jump when you realise that we have been here for around 200,000 years.

In a world where we have medication and immunisations on demand, Mother Nature cannot cull us to the extent to which she would like too. Therefore, we face a few issues going forward.

As global population rapidly increases, demand on already strained resources also increases. In order to find ways of meeting the global demand, I do not blame governments for approving such mass production. However, this again is done in vain as the root of the problem is not being addressed.

Being consciously aware that the inevitable will happen and that your efforts are in vain, if you knew that the dam wall was going to fall regardless of your efforts to slow it, would you still try to fill in the cracks? Darwin suggested that fittest survive, this being objective, regardless of rejecting human emotions.

Emotionally, the very suggestion of allowing Mother Nature to take her course appears evil. Logically, it seems like a wise idea. You see the conflict?

There are many that moan about life being unfair and twisted, full of conspiracy and out to get them. The truth is that life has never been easier. We have everything on demand to such an extent that we feel that we are entitled to such things.

Few will understand what I am trying to explain; I put this down to the majority being too engulfed in their vices to an extent where it is almost impossible to contemplate being without them. Like a spoilt child, reluctant to share even one of their many toys.

It is in this shortsightedness that has begun to strain resources. There are some examples that come to mind however I am sure that there are some many that this book would be too long.

Such things as hemp, we use cotton over hemp due to it yielding more financial fruit. Yet hemp takes one fifth of the time to grow, naturally contains its own pesticides where as cotton requires them to grow, hemp cleans the soil while cotton pollutes it, hemp removes carbon more successfully than cotton and hemp also has a substantial amount of uses over cotton.

Why don't we use hemp over cotton? Enter human greed... Powerful corporations saw how hemp would compete with their businesses. DuPont, along with The Bank Of Mellon and a journalist by the name of William Hearst set forth with one of the biggest propaganda campaigns one could imagine.

They knew that the many uses and ease of production of hemp would effect their investments and used everything in their power to outlaw the plant. Based on its herbal element (marijuana) it was declared public enemy number one. Interesting though, how in this modern day of connectivity, freedom of speech and access to history that we now realise this so much so, that in the modern day the plant can be legally smoked and its true benefits are widely accepted. Everything in moderation of course...

The point is that this material could have taken the world in a far better direction. Keeping fields fertile and the world a cleaner place it was an obvious route to take. History lessons to life lessons I suppose. The same concept could be said for Nikola Tesla's vision of free wireless energy for the world. But I wont go there…

Our world could have been very different to the one we know today. But that paradox was crushed like a bug under a foot. Some would argue that it was super necessary as big corporations provide much needed jobs. I agree, but if the world were put in a more natural state, then there would be enough jobs for all.

The natural order of things has been taken over by a very intelligent race. This again, is where the conflict between logic and emotion allows for a subtle conflict within even the most rational of minds. It's difficult to adopt a fresh new attitude to things whilst simultaneously dealing with this conflict. If perfection is but the ideals of and individual's perception of how something should be, then mass perfection will never be so.

I suppose the argument is to just roll with it and see where we end up as we, on a micro level can only make the changes in our own lives.

No one ever heard the scream of a single ant, but they were certainly aware of the march.

I often ponder actual things that we give value too. Diamonds, gold and money, I wonder what these things would be if we did not give them significance. Of course the concept of money in the form of a promise is a great idea. But like a drug, it's addictive and when people are addicted to something, they are capable of some crazy shit.

Although we empower these things, they are however, just things. Therefore significance is something that we gift to certain things to give them value. We become hypnotised by false values. What can we take from this in regard to our day-to-day lives? What really is worthy of significance? What if we was to give significance to what held most importance to the sustainability of life rather than things that just look nice?

The human mind itself is such a wonder. The ideas we have, the emotions we feel and the action put behind everything. It's something we truly should put value too. Wouldn't it be interesting if the implementation of science and technology were to be entrusted to the great minds that were able to produce the ideas rather than the big corporations that invested their dark money in to it? Just a thought…

It's difficult to not ponder the "what if's" in life. I supposed my mind just likes to wonder and it leads me to some interesting thoughts and questions. In reality this book was years in the making before I even knew that I was going to write it. But in doing so, it is definitely a relief of mind.

Now everything that goes on inside of my head, is out there. Out there for the world to read and with any luck, play a part in the necessary changes needed in society to make the world a better place.

Ultimately, the world will be here for a very long time and at this rate, far longer than we will be. But this will be at our own hand. The short-sighted choices that not only the governments of the world make, but us the people, make on a day to day basis are what will cement our future.

We are not living in a sustainable way and being ignorant to this is to be ignorant to the survival of our own species. The wellbeing of future generations depends on the choices we make going forward. A wake up call is needed on a global scale. A glimpse of the future state of society must be observed and understood by the masses. People learn in different ways, and by only speaking of the consequences is not enough.

Illustrations of our future world could push some that words do not get through too to make the necessary changes. This should be taught in school so that children have a good understanding of how society neglects the world and how they can make the changes needed to create a better world.

Everything comes down to education and awareness. Lack of education and awareness can often be misunderstood as ignorance, to which some believe is bliss, but in these circumstances, it is definitely not the case as the consequences for ignorance in the long term will be severe. As life ticks on for all of us in our day-to-day lives whilst living in the same routine, we find ourselves unaware as to what the future holds.

It is easy to see these problems as far too big and complex for you as an individual to make any change that would hold significance. However here lies the problem, as when millions of people have this same attitude as this, nothing will ever be done.

But as soon as people wake up to the realities of the current state of the world and the problems that we as humans create on an individual level, the sooner we can then all begin to reverse these problems on a scale that would make a significant difference. It is evident throughout history that we as a species have realised the fault in our ways and made the changes required for the better.

I do not see how this cannot be the case in this instance, especially when the consequences are worse than any before.

Many countries around the world have shown us that the changes needed are achievable. Iceland uses zero fossil fuels and are completely reliant on renewable energy sources that minimise carbon emissions. They source most of their food locally and have proven that the world can be made a better and cleaner place to live in.

There is a quiet war happening with the greedy of humanity and those that see the importance of long-term sustainability. A war where both sides are aware of the consequences of bleeding resources dry and using unsustainable energy mediums, however one side cares and the other pretends that they do whilst making endless excuses to continue with their dirty business so long as it keeps making them richer.

Effectively this accelerates the risk of us living in an unsustainable world, the powers that be are ignorant to this and power on with their agenda of regional domination. This is a shortsighted and stupid thing in hindsight. The only agenda that is crucial is that of sustainability.

Having the common people work together in order to achieve this is a near impossible task. Since the industrial revolution, convenience has gripped the masses and demand for more convenience feeds in to the greater problem of unsustainability. Products are created for our enjoyment and feed in to our emotional responses. Like a dog and its favourite toy, we will always be reluctant to lose it. We convince ourselves that we are dependent on modern technology.

This illusion is has fed the deterioration of our actual needs and in effect, who we are. It appears to me that humanity has lost touch with its senses and that we are shadows of our former selves. Our ability to think for ourselves has to some extent been polluted by the distractions of the cyber world.

Being creatures of a social disposition, we take to new technologies like a duck to water. The art of consumerism has led us to become dependent on things that we do not need. You don't burn your own home down to keep warm. Especially when you don't need too. Human nature is a remarkable thing and the sheer variation of people's nature is nuanced to such an extent that finding reason in the choices individuals make is a riddle in itself.

I do believe that people become their environments and the circumstances that they find themselves in lead them to do things that they would otherwise not do if better opportunity were present.

It is for the governments of the world to create opportunities for their people. These opportunities lead to jobs and an income. When people do not have opportunity, chaos can ensue, as the innate survival response is the number one priority.

With this in mind we can observe regions of the world where lack of opportunity is common and as a byproduct of this we will see heightened crime rates.

This divides communities and in effect creates dangerous areas to visit. Often we only see the reaction of problems and do not understand the catalyst.

I recently had a conversation with three people that helped me form a new opinion on a current world problem. There were six of us sitting at a table, socially. One of my good friends is a vegan, based on his passion for animals and their welfare and his deep sympathy for how many animals are mass-produced and how they are treated.

I feel that this is truly noble and I respect him for this. The two other people, like me, are consumers of meat and animal products.

The two other people were in complete agreement with my other friend in how awful it is that animals are treated in such a way. I quickly realised that there is a logical and emotional confliction present and I listened to each of their points.

Being something that I haven't given much thought too in the past, I did come to a stronger opinion that the mass production of animals is unfortunately relative. The issue is deeper than what it appears to be on the surface. I do not agree that animals should be treated in a manner that is cruel however the mass production of animal products does seem to hold relevance.

I have a couple of points that I would like to highlight. Those that hold platforms of a significant following tend to enjoy preaching ideals on how others should live and the choices others should make, yet the reasoning behind their push seems narrow minded and under researched.

Addressing an issue on face value is easy, but digging deeper in to the relativity of said problem seems to go a miss. Perhaps too laborious a task, or perhaps only appearing to be an advocate for something is the goal.

Firstly, as the population of the world continues to grow, the strain on resources will also have to grow. This is non-debatable, its just fact. The issue we have, is that we want our cake and to eat it too.

Meaning, as we have created vaccines and cures for so many of mother natures procedures of natural culling, human population has almost tripled in the last sixty years and bearing in mind, based on my own internal conflict between logic and emotion, I too am conflicted on this issue.

I see the issue but I wish no human to die, yet I know that if the population does continue to increase, we will inevitably need to find more ways to mass produce resources, creating more carbon emissions, thus making the world a less habitable place to live on.

So what do we do? This is a question that there will be no mass consensus.

The root of the problem is that there is just too many of us, and the number is growing rapidly.

"No one is hated more than he who speaks the truth"
- Plato.

People need to eat in order to survive. There is no fairness in nature and some things just are the way they are. We do not have to like it, it just is the way that it is. With this in mind, we can break down the face of the problem in to components in order to understand it on a deeper level. We cannot moan about the mass production of resources and yet be in favour of curing disease, its hypocritical.

The mass production is feeding the demand that we have created. Feeding the worlds hungry is what we all want to do. In doing so, we are feeding the original problem. It is not possible to feed the world on resources that are grown and farmed at the natural rate as they were intended to be. Getting back to veganism, I have no moral issue with it.

But I do see a logical issue with it. There are many pros to being a vegan, mostly regarding weight loss and a higher intake of micronutrients that the diet of many is deficient in. However, it is not the perfect diet. The macronutrient profiles between plants and animal products are different and serve different purposes within the body. Plant protein lacks some amino acids that are essential for the human body.

Not only this but the vegan diet can lead to a deficiency in calcium, omega-3 fatty acids, vitamin B-12 and folate which are all essential for the body. A long-term lack of these nutrients can have detrimental effects on the body. A question arises to me, being, if the body requires these essential nutrients, then how can a vegan diet be the correct way to eat? Just a thought…

Calcium is not only a mineral that keeps your bones and teeth healthy, it also allows your blood to clot and keeps your heart beating. Omega-3 fatty acids are essential for brain and heart health. Vitamin B-12 is known for its energy benefits but is also essential in keeping the body's blood and nerve cells healthy, it also helps to make DNA. Folate is needed to make red and white blood cells.

Folate also converts carbohydrates to energy and helps the body produce DNA and RNA. It is also essential for fetal growth. With all of this in mind, does a diet that includes meat sound like a bad thing?

Again, morally I understand why some vegans choose to be so. But I argue it is at there own peril based on the nutritional deficiencies in the long term. I understand that the core of the problem, being the mass production process will inevitably cause conflict for you, the reader too. But what is the solution?

This is where my push of understanding the difference between logic and emotion can be seen clearly. Life is full of these conflictions. To summarise, I have no argument with those who choose to be vegan.

I only wish to raise awareness on the sacrifice in being so and an understanding on why things are the way they are.

Chapter Ten

A Future Perspective

Many technologies when in their developmental stage were and are intended for good purposes, however many technologies are soon weaponised or selfishly held back from society so a plan of taxation or surveillance can be pre-formulated.

Some technologies are developed that have the capability of destroying human life as we know it, yet our elected officials neglected to call a vote from their people on whether or not we wanted these technologies in the first place.

Seeing as how they can impact the lives of the masses, I feel it shouldn't be up to the minority to make such decisions for the majority. I truly feel if the civilians of the world were to have had a vote, the nuclear bomb would not have existed.

Seeing as politicians are supposed to serve their people, perhaps they should run such things by their people.

For example, we are in the early years of artificial intelligence. My understanding of artificial intelligence has me both excited but at the same time I am very concerned. It is designed to mimic human intelligence. Artificial intelligence is constantly learning and attaining logic. My question is, what is logic without emotion?

And what will this mean for the human race if the world is one day governed by artificial intelligence?

A human mind in itself is an enigma and comes with a plethora of variables. Can we teach human emotion? Can we teach a machine to feel? I guess this is history of things to come.

This is a very important question, especially when allowing artificial intelligence access to sensitive data. Artificial intelligence may be able to do great things for us, but I feel we must restrict it.

Without emotion, logic is chaos. Without logic, emotion is chaos. The balance must be consistent.

The effects of a less serious imbalance between the two are evident in every day life. Logic would suggest that a lower global populace would be resourcefully beneficial for the human race, however emotion would dictate that human life is to be sustained regardless overpopulation.

What would the logic of artificial intelligence be? What priorities would we entrust artificial intelligence with? If artificial intelligence had access to a national defense system, how would it implement its logic in regard to the global population struggles we will one day face? These are my concerns.

I do feel artificial intelligence would hold benefits in some fields, especially in the distant future, fields such as medicine, law & order, health care, infrastructure, climate predictions and space exploration.

Although I am conflicted, my concerns are only a reflection of the ripples of history showing us how Mankind has a tendency to weaponise new technologies. In doing so, corrupting the original hopes and visions of the minds of scientific pioneers.

For example, nuclear energy could have been such a testament to human evolution. But, it had to be weaponised and used to destroy life rather than to accommodate it. This is an insult to the scientific world. I digress...

Upon discovering new worlds that are within reach and in a habitable zone that humans could one day occupy, artificial intelligence could be used to locate and notify us of such places. We could send long-life robots equipped with artificial intelligence to these planets where they could conduct risk assessments and gather data, which would otherwise be difficult to obtain within a human lifespan.

The truth is that the only option for the prolonged continuum of the human race is for us to become an interplanetary species.

I often stood in Dubai Marina, leaning on the guardrail, hypnotized whilst staring up at the skyscrapers under the night sky, The Cayan Tower, Marina Gate, Princess Tower and The Torch. All lit up, standing tall evocatively, like huge futuristic rockets about to set off in to space, carrying humans to new worlds, never to return. That may read crazy or be hard to comprehend, but perhaps one day it will be a reality, especially if the continuum of the species is dependent upon it. I presume the future will tell all, but of course not in my lifetime.

The choices of those that are in control are what will dictate our future, an agenda of a few that has a lasting effect on the masses. It is whether or not those leaders have an agenda for the betterment and prosperity of mankind that is important.

As we march forward in to this new era of human habitat, I ponder many aspects of the circumstances of our lives, as digital worlds replace the tangible worlds of individuals. Hours on end locked in to a virtual reality of ones and zeros.

Is this actual fulfillment or is it a synthetic happiness to fill a void? As the entropy of life succumbs to disorder, will there be a generation of people in regret in their final days?

Money, sex and power dictate the narrative. We live in a society where anything necessary is done in order to acquire these things. What of moral value and logic?

As time has moved forward and technologies have advanced, humanity now worships idols based on their following and like count, a sad world where reality is suspended for that of the digital.
Your means of interpreting your world are misused in these parameters and can lead to no long-term happiness.

I often feel as though I am standing outside of life, looking in and observing the madness within. Follie á Deux.

They say that history does not repeat itself, but that it rhymes. We live today in a world where the human need is the same as ever. All that has changed is the evolution of mediums to obtain that mental fulfillment. What has become stagnant is the human ability to abstain from excess.

It is eagerly believed that fulfillment is obtained by material gain. Ad nauseam. The emotional connection to this belief renders people predictable. The foundation of humanity is in the ability to absorb. What you absorb will dictate your being.

Someone once said to me that time is an illusion. It didn't quite sit well in my mind. Entropy is relative to time, so we know that time exists. The second law of thermodynamics uses time as its medium for gradual disorder. Time exists. What time is often confused with is consciousness.

Consciousness is simultaneous. All that ever exists is this present moment. Time is linear and consciousness is simultaneous. Learning to differentiate between the two offers clarity.

The opinions of the masses will never align. We never all agree on everything, as perspective is subjective. Meaning, that we can always learn something from everyone that we meet. The need not only to be right, but the need to project it has faded for me.

I, like many of us have fucked up many of times in life. But I have learned that this is relative to our becoming. Reality has hit in recent times and my perspective on many things has changed. To be truly present in every moment has offered clarity in life, even for a man of many minds.

In this present time, humanity is crawling out of the Covid-19 era and in to a new world. As I go for my early morning walk in the back streets of old London, the cold always reminds me that I am alive. It offers clarity of thought and new perspective to be formed.

Thinking logically, in a world where many jobs have been; and many more are soon to be taken by machines, coupled with the knowledge that human population has almost tripled in the last sixty years, would it be incredibly awful of me to suggest logically that Covid-19 is natures answer to human over-population?

Trying to mitigate the spread of a viral disease is the same as filling in the cracks of a dam wall that is about to burst. We may not like it, but it is the inevitable.

Throughout nature, all species have a natural volume cap. For our own species, implementing on-mass, medical and scientific advancements has interrupted this cap. The healthy and natural advancement of a species is achieved by natural protocols.

Regardless of emotional based rejection, this evidently just so happens to be the logical case. Jenner developed the first vaccine for small pox in 1796 and up until that point no disease wiped out humanity. Heard immunity prevailed and our species was replenished to a healthy population.

In two million years up until 1796, humanity was naturally becoming stronger. Now, our strength is based on synthetic mediums to prolong life. This is almost a cheat code in some cases, as many are in positions of poor health by their own doing.

I know that last paragraph read quite savagely, but in suspending emotion from time to time, we can acquire some harsh but necessary truths. The only thing on this earth that has the potential to wipe out humanity is humanity itself through war and greed.

Heard immunity is relative and essential. What is not is forcefully limiting peoples quality of life for something that is inevitable. There is no panacea for mother natures will. Food for thought…

On the subject of war, it is said that democracy was invented in order to avoid warfare. We live in a world where the will of the people is seldom observed. World leaders quarrel with each other, using the pawns of society as their cannon fodder on the front lines.

The common people, who would in most circumstances be at peace if it were not for political jousting, are slammed together under a false rhetoric as though they are natural enemies when they are not. It is the politicians that are at war, yet the cowardice they convey by using their citizens to fight their battles will forever live in my mind as shameful.

The power truly is with the people but yet this power is unobtainable as the emotions of the people are hijacked by propaganda leading to fear and civil unrest. In most cases the fight for peace is a false flag, the real agenda being exploitation in which ultimately feeds that human need control in the forms of money, sex and power.

The leaders of the world are limited by their myopic scope on human preservation, blindsided by their emotional needs. The same psychology as gang culture applies to the countries of the world, each in it for themselves on a micro level, at the expense of others. Yet the potential achievements of mankind as a whole if a unified global agenda was established, is almost unimaginable.

Allies, nuclear weapons, spying and assassinations are part of an agenda the every day person of the masses does not want. Freedom, peace and unity are only unattainable because the masses allow it to be so.

We step forward in to the future, a world that is changing. The environmental damages mankind has made becoming more so evident as the rhythm of the seasons has become dramatically effected.

The planet will be fine but indeed we will be at its mercy. With the gradual onset of renewables and clean energy, I cannot help but ponder how this will change the dynamic of world order. As our reliance on fossil fuels draws away, the providers of these mediums scramble to invest in new long-term resources.

Countries again, jousting for a dominant position in the new world dynamic as resources needed to supply our new renewable world are subject to global politics, again something beautiful, mercilessly corrupted by mankind.

Australia, Chile, China and Argentina are countries with incredibly dense lithium reserves. With China owning resource assets in Australia and Chile it would appear that the Chinese powerhouse will indeed hold its power for a long time to come.

The democratic republic of the Congo has the largest Cobalt deposits in the world. Cobalt is essential for the production of direct current batteries in electric vehicles.

According to the New York Times, As of last year, 15 of the 19 cobalt-producing mines in Congo were owned or financed by Chinese companies, according to a data analysis by The Times and Benchmark Mineral Intelligence.

The biggest alternative to Chinese operators is Glencore; a Switzerland-based company that runs two of the largest cobalt mines there.

China is also the largest producer of manganese in the world. The irony is that a country that has built its wealth on mass production and mass use of fossil fuels holds the reigns for the production of the future we need as a species.

I can only imagine that going forward, space exploration will be under the guise of finding new habitable worlds to elongate the survival of our species, but in reality, more so to exploit the natural resources in which they yield.

I imagine a new space race, one where world leaders bicker for control of new worlds and their resources. I pray that this is not at the cost of the lives of every day people, coerced in to fighting a war that was never theirs.

I imagine space wars; I imagine the race for these technologies will lead to developments in technologies that are inconceivable to the modern mind. As I pay attention to scientific advancements around the world I am drawn to the developments of fusion technology currently being spear headed in China.

Successful tests that will inevitably one day lead to machines that can travel great distances and propel mankind in to a new age. We are only in the early hours of this new dawn in human capability. A sad thought creeps in to my mind, what of art, culture and all that it is to be human?

The everyday person walks life in a parallel with those that will give birth to a new age of discovery, the finite idea of life for the latter but the precious beauty of every moment for the former.

In this sense I wonder if what asked on page eight is a question for myself or the reader, would you rather be involuntarily aware of everything going on around you, or live in the peaceful bubble of ignorance?

There is so much to observe from history, from this present moment and going forward in to the future. So much that it is often like a loud noise I wish I could turn down.

I am excited to see what the future brings, but for now my contentment lays within this present moment.

Chapter Eleven

Love

Love is the only thing that makes sense, even without words. The strongest of all human emotion and that which defies all logic but yet creates its own.

There are many forms of love. Family, friendship, romantic and self love are just to name a few, each evoking a deep sense of connection, but yet so very different from each other in their own indescribable way.

You should always endeavour to be great on your own, more than great, you have to be full and whole in your own company to the point where you are utterly content. Love yourself first. There is a stark difference between being alone and lonely.

Like and emotional wrecking ball, many troubled souls go from person to person, trying to fill the void in themselves that will never be filled by theses means.

Pretending to be someone that they are not in order to run away from who they really are.

We often think of love, as it is portrayed in film and books, however this is not always a reality. Love is that of compromise, courage and the adaptable.

Humans are they apex in making excuses for themselves. As civilized as we have become, we are still in the jungle and there is no fairness in nature.
This is survival of the fittest and no amount of excuses will save you from the truth within, that you face when no one else is around. You must ground yourself and feel internal balance and acceptance before you can understand another.

Your personal ideals are irrelevant in the wild. You do not control nature, as you are merely part of it. Life begins when you relinquish your control. Acceptance of what is, is what harbours peace of mind. Idealism is that of the dreamer. Adaptation is that of the brave and wise.

True friendship is a blessing, a beautiful form of love and a connection between two people where both just want the other to be successful and happy, trust and laughter, comparison of experience and endless life lessons. It is nice to have someone in your corner.

I've been lucky enough to make a few friends in life from many different backgrounds. Sharing experiences and life lessons with me that have been invaluable in forming who I am today. In Swedish there is a word "Fika" which literally means, lets go for coffee. I love this. It expresses that genuine want for social interaction and conversation.

I learned a lot about Scandinavian culture over the years and just seeing that one word can mean so much was astonishing to me. In Danish the word "Hygge" literally meaning finding joy in every day moments and practicing mindfulness. In one word.

Having some much meaning behind a word to summarise a feeling is beautiful. Observable in this is what it is to be human. Language has taught me more than words. It has taught me that regardless of the sound we make with our mouths, the message is the same.

Through all of the emotional highs and lows of human life, the one emotion that supersedes everything is love. Love has the ability to change everything and is the only thing that makes sense in life. Rare it is in its true form and often falsely declared or misunderstood.

A locking of eyes can shudder your world and feel as though time has stopped. As though the energy between you and another has interconnected.

A first kiss can feel as though electricity is flowing through your body. How powerful an emotion to have such physical effects on the body. The world itself feels brighter and your reality glows. You feel every breath you take and life has an ambiance to it.

Many have written about love and in turn many have read about love. Most songs, movies and shows are based on love to which many find themselves with high hopes of love. And why not, why would you not want the most beautiful feeling in the world?

You see this is where logic can be applied to love. In the creation of yearning for love we can fall in to a false sense of expectation.
We can apply these expectations on to new people we meet and become disappointed when things did not go as expected.

Things do not always go the way of the movies or songs. Often, love is unexpected. It is but our human impatience and expectation that forces things to go as we expect them to, like forcing a square cog through a circular hole.

We are hardwired to feel. Many are in love with the idea of being in love so much so that they apply their full self in to a false sense of love that was never there to be reciprocated. This is why love is rare. Occurring through a natural means rather than false means is hard to achieve when you have a preexisting expectation on how things should go.

If you over-water your plant in the hope that it will grow faster, its life will only run its course to a premature and disappointing end. Regardless of how pure your intentions were.

Do not tell yourself that you're looking for a relationship and to the same end, do not tell yourself that you're not. Both attitudes create a false sense of expectation. You're forcing an outcome that goes against nature. As though you are surfing the wave of life, just go with it and let your intuition guide you over your emotional biases.

Love is beautiful and love is life. Love is also blind and it is not to be governed by Man, as it is that lent by nature to Mankind as a gift.
Connections are relative to humanity and have no rules when pure. Preference is subjective and love is love.

Gay people have been in existence throughout history. Great leaders and some of the greatest minds in history have been of such nature. To whom without, our world would be a far different and a less knowledgeable place. Branded as disgusting, unholy and sinful by other men throughout history who deem themselves worthy enough to dictate whom one can love.

If God created such people, then how may anyone sworn to God contradict his will? Hypocrisy, as you will see from my various observations have been prevalent throughout this book.

We must never change who we are, particularly for the approval of others. In some cases compromise is necessary, particularly in relationships or with family. But we must choose our partners based on the enrichment they bring to our lives and vice versa.

In this modern day where the world is saturated with options through the heavy amounts of popular dating applications, what does this take away from the ability to have a strong relationship? So spoiled with options that any potential relationship gained may not be appreciated to the same extent as if the two met outside of the cyber world in a natural manner.

The demographic of people between the ages of 21 and 30 years old is usually where the problems are by my observation. Those prime years where people tend to meet their life partners seem to be corrupted by the way technology has influenced the agendas of people.

Whilst writing this book I have had a lot of open conversations with people in an attempt to expand my mind. Many of those conversations that I've had with women tend to revolve around the same things in regard to what men do to irritate or upset them. Most of it is in regard to commitment. For instance, they meet a guy and they message each other for a while.

He takes her out and is the nicest guy to her, but the moment they've slept with each other he starts to go quiet, leaving her feeling used and frustrated. Of course, it is in the nature of a young man to get around, as it were.

Which there is nothing wrong with. But when doing so, if the impression that is given to the girl is that he is emotionally invested in her, just so he can sleep with her, I think this is wrong. It's a cheap approach.

There does come a point where we all are looking for more. Having a deeper relationship with someone can be the most fulfilling feeling. I'd argue that women understand this more than men. Throughout history women have had to endure more pain than men, both physically and mentally. I feel that this has made women emotionally superior to men.

Women have learned to process emotions in such a way that a man just simply couldn't comprehend it. Men are simple when it comes to emotions and I believe this can be a frustration for women.

Men do not like to take emotional chances and when they do, they put all of their eggs in one basket and feel that their person is the source of their happiness, when in truth, their person is only part of their happiness.

This can be a dangerous path and can lead the man to making some emotionally based decisions that can make him come across too intense or weak. Which is not ideal. This is a good example of where men are not as evolved emotionally as women. You must always remember to be yourself. A relationship should be like a Venn diagram, two over-lapping circles. To the left and right you are yourselves as individuals and the person that the other fell for, but you always meet in the middle.

A lot of female heartbreak comes from falling for a man that is not yet emotionally ready to commit and in not being so, does things that cause pain to the woman. I am in no way making excuses for men behaving like a pig.

I am shining a light on their nature to frolic around with their heightened testosterone levels and lack of readiness to find something deeper.

It is in the nature of a lot of men to be this way. My advice to women is to read the signs early and not be too naive in their thinking that they can change this mans nature when he is not ready for it to be changed.

Once a man does fall, he will fall hard and you will feel it. Do not settle for less and realise that all relationships are a maintenance job, even the ones that seem perfect.

It's important to not lose your identity when falling in love, as love is not about changing who you are.

Compromising is essential as you are two different people, which will not see everything in the same way. A healthy relationship is like a Venn diagram, two overlapping circles that meet each other in the middle. You fell for the person you met, and they you. Never lose yourself and your love will be forever beautiful.

The harsh realities of life, being that it ends, is what makes life forever beautiful. But one thing is for sure, and that is that it wouldn't hurt to have more love in the world.